THE GRAND UNION CANAL WALK

THE GRAND UNION CANAL WALK

*Walkers heading north while the boaters go south near Bridge 65,
The Navigation Inn*

THE GRAND UNION CANAL WALK
London to Birmingham

by
Clive Holmes

CICERONE PRESS
MILNTHORPE, CUMBRIA

© Clive Holmes 1996
ISBN 1 85284 206 7
A catalogue record for this book is available from the British Library.

DEDICATION
For Daniel

ACKNOWLEDGEMENTS

I would like to thank Malcolm, Chris and Nick for their company during the first stage of this route, but above all my thanks are due to my wife Kathleen for her companionship along the whole route. It was a long walk but one we will always remember; we walked it together.

Cicerone Books by the same author: Cotswold Walks (3 volumes)

Front Cover: Canal museum at Stoke Bruerne

CONTENTS

Introduction 9
   Using the Guide 10
   Practical Points 10
   Walking the Towpath 11
   Accommodation and Public Transport 12
   Maps 12
   An Outline History of the Grand Union Canal 12

Route
   Stage 1: Little Venice, London to Bulls Bridge 13 miles 15
   Stage 2: Bulls Bridge to Harefield 8$^{1}/_{4}$ miles 24
   Stage 3: Harefield to Apsley 12$^{1}/_{2}$ miles 32
   Stage 4: Apsley to Bulbourne 13 miles 43
   Stage 5: Bulbourne to Three Locks 9$^{1}/_{2}$ miles 51
   Stage 6: Soulbury Three Locks to Gifford Park 11$^{1}/_{2}$ miles 59
   Stage 7: Gifford Park, Milton Keynes to Stoke Bruerne
            12$^{1}/_{2}$ miles 66
   Stage 8: Stoke Bruerne to Weedon 12$^{1}/_{4}$ miles 80
   Stage 9: Weedon to Braunston 9$^{1}/_{2}$ miles 86
   Stage 10: Braunston to Radford Semele 13$^{1}/_{2}$ miles 92
   Stage 11: Radford Semele to Shrewley 10 miles 99
   Stage 12: Shrewley to Catherine de Barnes 10 miles 104
   Stage 13: Catherine de Barnes to Gas Street, Birmingham
            12 miles 110

Useful Addresses 118
Bibliography 119

THE GRAND UNION CANAL WALK

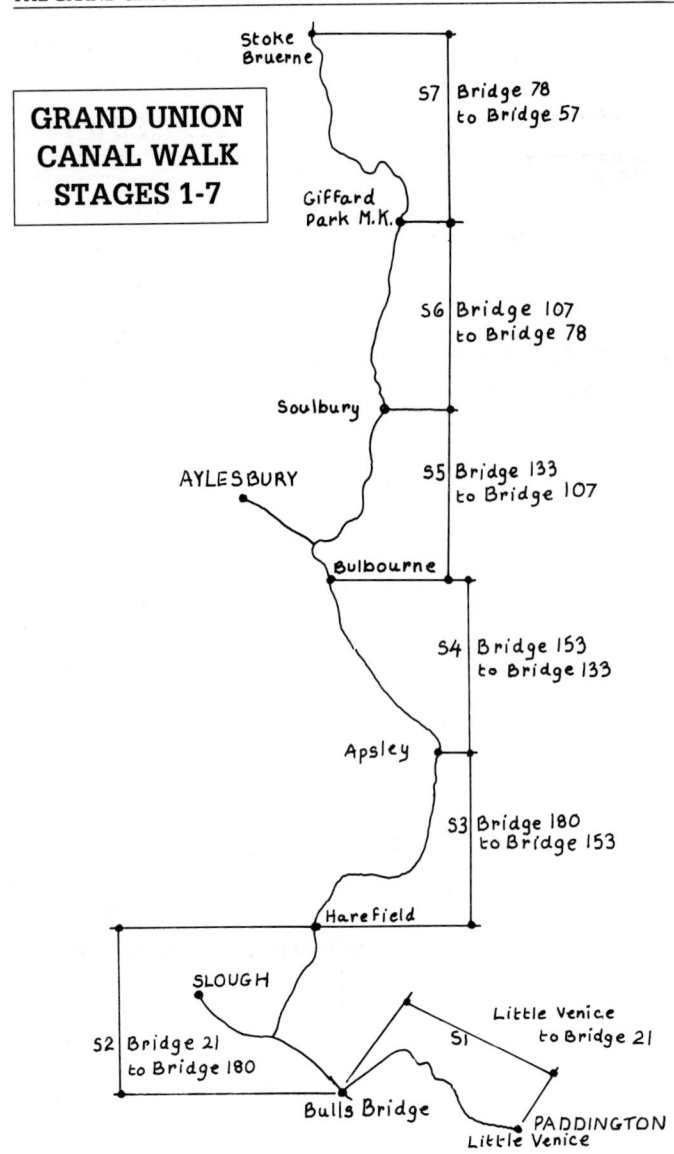

GRAND UNION CANAL WALK STAGES 1-7

- Stoke Bruerne
- S7 Bridge 78 to Bridge 57
- Giffard Park M.K.
- S6 Bridge 107 to Bridge 78
- Soulbury
- AYLESBURY
- S5 Bridge 133 to Bridge 107
- Bulbourne
- S4 Bridge 153 to Bridge 133
- Apsley
- S3 Bridge 180 to Bridge 153
- Harefield
- SLOUGH
- S2 Bridge 21 to Bridge 180
- S1 Little Venice to Bridge 21
- Bulls Bridge
- PADDINGTON Little Venice

6

GRAND UNION CANAL WALK STAGES 8-13

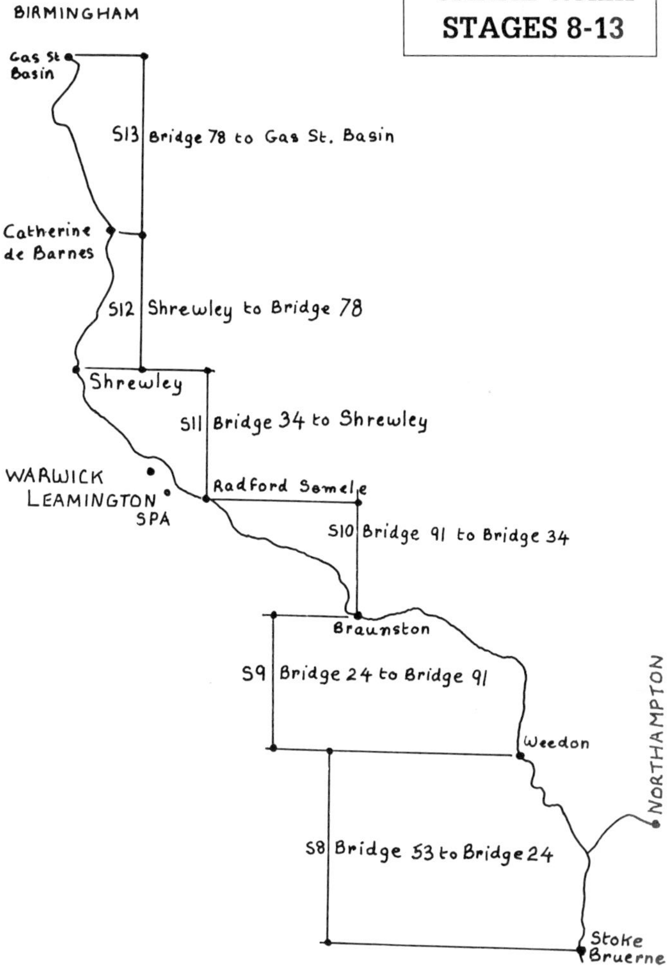

KEY TO ROUTE DETAILS
and facilities on or near the towpath

- ▬▬▬ Canal with towpath
- - - - - Alternative Route
- ⇥)(⇤ 53 Canal bridge with number
- ▬▬┼▬▬ L Canal with lock and towpath
- GS. General store
- PH. Public house
- CP. Car park
- PT. Public telephone
- M Marina
- PO. Post office
- PS. Picnic site

INTRODUCTION

The 200th anniversary of the birth of the various canals, which from 1929 formed the Grand Union complex, was celebrated by the official opening of England's newest long distance trail on 9th July 1993. I had walked from Little Venice in London to Stoke Bruerne in separate stages early in the summer and chose to walk from Stoke Bruerne to Gas Street, Birmingham, as a backpacking exercise during August.

After spending so much time walking in the Cotswolds for my trilogy of books, I relished the complete contrast of the Grand Union Canal walk. After all, its highest point near Daventry being only about 600ft above the Thames. Of course it had to be that way in order that it should flow along the most level route from London to the Midlands.

It is therefore an ideal route for those who wish to get their head down and batter their way along the 147 or so miles in five or six days, just as it is ideal for those who wish to take a more leisurely pace and explore as they go. Whichever of the two methods you choose to adopt you will never be too far from civilization where accommodation, provisions, toilets and places to eat and drink are available.

For most people there is a strange fascination about walking alongside water; for me the coast is the ideal, with river walks next, but the whole length of the Grand Union Canal with its unending changes of scenery proved to be full of fascination and interest. Each of the thirteen sections described is rich in history, architecture - old and new - in addition to the ever changing plant, bird and wildlife.

Constructed by the engineers of the 18th and early 19th centuries the canals, together with their immediate surroundings, have become a natural habitat for wildlife with rabbits, foxes, voles, numerous dragonflies and butterflies, ducks, swans, mallard, moorhen, heron and coot never too far away. The anglers you will meet will be patiently waiting at the end of their fishing lines for signs of perch, roach, bream, carp, tench and gudgeon.

Once away from London's suburbs the canal delves into lesser known parts of England, parts that were rarely visited because in the past this part of England was only known to those who lived and worked along the canal. This, then, is England at its most secretive, a part of the country that has lain hidden, disregarded and almost unwanted after its commercial life was over until fairly recent times. Now it is a part of this country's industrial history and unspoilt countryside which is being preserved so that we and future generations can enjoy this canal that zig-zags its way through more than 200 years of heritage. Some people will choose to explore it from the water; I chose the towpath.

USING THE GUIDE
In writing and illustrating this book I have aimed to produce a guide that is interesting as well as informative for those who wish to walk the whole route and for those who wish to walk only parts of it.

The contents are laid out in two parts:
(1) The Route
(2) Places and Points of Interest Along the Way

(1) The Route is indicated by a series of maps for each of the thirteen sections of the journey. On each map clear details and instructions regarding the journey along the towpath are given. Since I walked the towpath from south to north I have written the instructions and drawn the maps to read in the same direction, i.e. from the bottom of the page to the top.

(2) Places and Points of Interest Along the Way contains information about the towns, villages and places through which the canal passes, together with those within close proximity to the canal.

PRACTICAL POINTS
There will inevitably be people who, like me, wish to walk the whole route. For this purpose I have divided the journey into thirteen sections or stages that can reasonably be covered in a full day's walk, allowing some time to explore. If, however, you wish to get along quicker it is easy to do so as there are ample places to join and leave the towpath. Alternatively, you may decide to walk shorter distances with children and spend more time exploring the surrounding areas. Towpath walking is above all else flexible but you still need to do some advance planning.

I walked all the stages from Little Venice to Stoke Bruerne at different times, sometimes taking a car to the finish then motoring with another vehicle to the start, walking the stage then collecting the vehicles as appropriate. On other occasions I motored to the nearest railway station, took the train to the start, walked the stage and collected my car on completion. To walk the stages from Stoke Bruerne to Gas Street I decided to backpack and pre-book bed and breakfast accommodation which, since the accommodation list supplied by British Waterways was somewhat sparse, was not an easy task. Hopefully as time progresses there will be a greater number of bed and breakfast establishments within a reasonable distance of the canal. These then are the alternative methods I used but with additional resources such as youth hostels, campsites and buses the alternatives are numerous.

Some people, notably those who lack walking experience, are under the misconception that the average person walks at 4 miles per hour, however only the young and the fit will keep to this pace. The average walker carrying a full pack will find that $2^{1/4}$ miles an hour is far more realistic if any sightseeing is to be undertaken en route.

WALKING THE TOWPATH

This route passes through some very attractive and lesser known parts of the English countryside but it also passes through some derelict industrial landscapes. This is certainly so for much of the final stage as it climbs into the old industrial centre of Birmingham. Here, however, whilst there is still much to be done, improvement has already been made to the towpath and its surroundings. The start at Little Venice is quite agreeable and the towpath surface for almost all of this first stage is the best you will get until you approach Milton Keynes in Buckinghamshire, so make the most of it. Once a few miles clear of the start some stretches of the canal are quite isolated with much decay and dereliction, the London Canals Committee therefore advises that you do not walk alone on the city's towpaths. Apart from the surface little has been done as yet to make the towpath more interesting for the walker; let us hope that some of the effort being made in Birmingham will filter through to the capital in the future.

Finally, whilst dealing with the towpath, in spite of the claims by British Waterways that it is walkable for the whole route, it isn't yet! The area near Napton in Northamptonshire has for years been in a very poor state of repair and whilst work is in hand to upgrade it, at the time of writing I would suggest that you follow the alternative route using public rights of way.

ACCOMMODATION AND PUBLIC TRANSPORT
When planning the walking of any long distance trail it is obvious that the accommodation required is as close as possible to the route being followed and it is as well to emphasize this point when enquiring about accommodation.

Accommodation along the Grand Union Canal Walk is available from British Waterways, The Stop House, Braunston, Northants NN11 7JQ. Tel: 01788 890666. Price £1.50p.

Throughout the length of the canal the towpath is never more than a couple of miles away from public transport of some kind.

To reach Uxbridge, Rickmansworth and Watford use the Metropolitan Railway Line of London Transport and for Uxbridge or Alperton use the Piccadilly Line. King's Langley, Apsley, Hemel Hempstead, Berkhamstead, Tring, Leighton Buzzard and Milton Keynes all lie along the main line of the British Rail network from Euston to Rugby. Hatton, Lapworth, Solihull, Olton, Acocks Green, Tyseley and Bordesley can be reached by using the Birmingham Snowhill line to Leamington Spa.

MAPS
I have prepared this book in such a way that you will require no other sources of information to guide you from Little Venice to Gas Street Basin. If, on the other hand, you plan to make side trips from the towpath of distances of more than a few miles the right map is indispensable. The main canal route and its immediate surrounding countryside are covered by the Ordnance Survey Landranger series with a scale of 1:50,000 Nos. 139, 151, 152, 165, 166 and 176. Should you require greater details the relevant Pathfinder series with a scale of 1:25,000 should be consulted.

AN OUTLINE HISTORY OF THE GRAND UNION CANAL
The companies that amalgamated in 1929 to form the Grand Union Canal Company were the inherent companies of those that had existed in various sizes and degrees of profitability since the early days of England's canals. Long before 1929 a canal route to London

from the Midlands had existed using the Birmingham and Fazeley Canal, and later the Coventry and Oxford Canal provided the way from Birmingham to Oxford. From here goods were transported on the Thames to London. This route, something of a 'round the houses' circuit, was finished during 1790 with a tremendous development in trading during the following years.

At this time Britain was once again trying to regain its financial feet after losing the very expensive War of Independence with the young nation of America. The demand for all manner of manufactured goods, with the consequent requirement for the transportation of raw materials, meant that a more efficient system, i.e. a more direct route, had to be developed.

One must remember that at that time the only method of transporting anything in bulk was by using horse power. It was clearly far more efficient to use the horse to tow a loaded canal barge than it was to expect the animal to pull a fraction of the same weight in a cart along a road. As a result the canals became the main traffic routes for all kinds of bulky and heavy materials and could be likened to our present-day trunk roads and motorways.

The chance of vast profits attracted huge investment by the rich, and various canal companies sprung up all over the country. This period in history is still referred to as the years of 'canal mania'. Some of these canals were five-minute wonders, improperly thought through and never finished; others fizzled out after a short period of trading. Other companies who had constructed canals using well conceived routes providing strong links between centres of commerce and industry were more successful.

During the late 1700s Birmingham was emerging as something of a 'boom town'; it had already proved itself during earlier times as a manufacturer of munitions to the armies of Cromwell. Now it was developing in engineering, forging, pressing and stamping in addition to other methods of manufacturing metal items from simple clasps to heavy machinery.

In 1793 an Act of Parliament was passed which authorised the commencement of work on the canal known as the Grand Junction. It was to be built from the Oxford Canal at Braunston down to the Thames at Brentford. It was to have several branches, the most important of which linked it up to Paddington, right at the centre of London. It was truly an imaginative project! Almost immediately

Birmingham was 'canal linked' to Warwick, by 1794 to Napton and then to Braunston; thus the main artery of the Grand Union was in place.

Previously the canals were excavated to take boats 7ft (2.1m) wide and were equipped with locks that could cope with boats with a length ten times their width, but these new direct routes were equipped with locks to take boats of double the old width. The exception to this thinking was in the Midlands close to Birmingham, the very centre of the manufacturing industries, where the existing canal companies resisted any suggestion of widening. This philosophy was their mistaken way of protecting their trade but eventually it only helped in their demise.

The whole network was finally completed in 1805, a tremendous achievement when you consider that it was built using only gunpowder for blasting, together with the pick, shovel, horse and cart. Incidentally, this was the same year in which the Battle of Trafalgar was fought.

From 1805 the canals prospered for barely 30 years, then, as the development of the steam-powered locomotive gathered speed, and with the expansion of the railway companies, the canal trade waned.

By 1929 time had almost run out for the independent canal companies, partially due to their own complacency over a long period of time and primarily due to the development of the railways and the invention of the internal combustion engine. The heady days of high profits were long since gone and almost as a last-ditch stand the Grand Junction Canal Company, the Regents Canal Company and the other companies that owned the canals between Birmingham and Napton, became one. Thus, the Grand Union was formed, controlling more than 270 miles of waterway. During the early 1930s many of the narrow locks were updated between Napton and Birmingham with the aid of finances from the Government, and resulted in the route from Birmingham to London all having wide locks. The complete modernisation was declared open by the Duke of Kent at Hatton Locks in 1934; this updating was to prove itself many times over during the Second World War. Since then the canals have had various owners but in 1962 they were all transferred to the British Waterways Board and since 1968 the Grand Union has been developed primarily for pleasure traffic.

STAGE 1:
Little Venice to Bulls Bridge

PLACES AND POINTS OF INTEREST ALONG THE WAY

Little Venice

Today Little Venice is one of the most pleasant and best known areas of London's canals. Its quiet, rather up-market atmosphere contrasts sharply with its past history when it was the very centre of the old Regents Canal and the Paddington arm of the Grand Union Canal, busy with commercial traffic.

It has a certain pedigree - the poet Robert Browning resided at close-by Warwick Crescent for 25 years from 1862 and the triangular-shaped piece of water, with its tree-clad island, at the junction of the canals is known as Brownings Pool. Nowadays the brightly painted and well polished house boats moored alongside are home, if only for part of the year, to a handful of well-known personalities.

Close by is Paddington Basin which was opened in 1801. This changed the former quiet parish of rural Paddington for all time to become the only canal with wharfing facilities in the nation's capital city. Nineteen years later the Regents Canal was completed and nowadays it is a very elegant stretch of tree-lined waterway overlooked by gracious houses.

From Little Venice our route takes us below Westbourne Terrace and past the British Waterways Canal office which, during the canal's commercial heyday, was the Toll Office. It was positioned so that its occupants had a good view over the narrows as the barges squeezed through and the vessel's gauge was measured to assess the necessary toll.

The sophistication of our starting place is soon left behind as the first stage of our long walk gets under way, passing through some of the vast industrial areas of central London. Soon after bridge No.5 the huge gasometers of Kensal Town are passed on the left, then on the right is the cemetery - quiet and peaceful. From Kensal Green, close to bridge No.6, familiar landmarks are visible such as Wormwood Scrubs prison, the Post Office Tower and Queens Park Rangers football ground. Next come the vast railway sidings and

THE GRAND UNION CANAL WALK

Little Venice, London

STAGE 1 - LITTLE VENICE TO BULLS BRIDGE

the unending industrial area, then Willesden Junction railway station followed by Harlesden. This is still London's outskirts amidst decaying industrial grime.

Park Royal

Park Royal is where much of the munitions were manufactured during the First World War and is today still well known as a large manufacturing area.

The Acton Power Station, built at the end of the Second World War, is easily visible. Also you will recognise the McVities, Heinz and Guinness factories. The latter's premises of 1936 is regarded by some as one of Sir Gilbert Scott's architectural masterpieces. Four huge brick-built blocks form the main building surrounded by a series of smaller buildings and green lawns.

Horsenden Hill

After bridge No.12 the Sudbury Golf Course comes into view and after a left-hand bend in the canal the wooded Horsenden Hill, all 270ft plus of it, can be seen to the right. Fine views from this vantage point are possible and it is claimed that Windsor Castle, Sydenham and Highgate are some of the places that can be seen on a clear day.

Northolt

Soon the canal twists through Northolt where Glaxo, Mothers Pride, Lyons and Tetley's all have premises. The old Northolt Airport is about half a mile away to the north. It was built very quickly and efficiently in 1915 for the forerunner of the Royal Air Force, the Royal Flying Corps, and expanded at a tremendous pace. It was a Fighter Command base during the Battle of Britain and perhaps reached its peak of fame during late September 1940 when the Luftwaffe attempted to demolish it. A wing of the Polish Air Force was based at Northolt during those dark days and a monument to their losses is topped by a large eagle. Northolt is used today mainly by transport aircraft of the RAF as Heathrow has taken over the commercial traffic.

Southall

Southall is another area of back to back terraced houses and diverse industries. The old Great Western Railway came here in 1839 and since then the whole district has expanded rapidly. I recall that it used to be the home of AEC, the builder of heavy vehicles and of the famous London buses before they became part of the Leyland Group. Today EMI and Wimpey are well established here. As a result of settling in Southall during the last 20 years or so many immigrant families provide the work-force for the numerous processed food factories that abound, along with the traditional industries.

Denham

After bridge No.182 about ¾ mile due west of the towpath Denham Court can be found at the end of the cottage-lined main street of Denham village. It was here that the Jacobean poet John Dryden wrote *Ode to the Feast of St Cecilia*. The church of St Mary's at the end of the drive to Denham Court, contains many Elizabethan monuments amongst which is a brass to Henry VIII's Master of the Mint, Sir Edmund Peckham, who had much to do with generating the prosperity of that period. The stone and flint tower dates from Norman times.

Denham is now part of Greater London but remains an attractive village with its historical church and village architecture - an oasis within suburbia.

STAGE 1 - LITTLE VENICE TO BULLS BRIDGE

Bridge No.6 is quickly followed by a railway bridge and the canal passes between industrial units and railway yards.

STAGE 1:
Little Venice to Bulls Bridge
Map: Landranger 176
Start: GR. Q 261 818
Distance: 13 miles

Immediately after the Harrow Road bridge the M40 briefly forms a cover for the towpath as it skims overhead and off to the left. The towpath follows the canal to the right.

At Little Venice join the towpath from Delemere Terrace where the bridge crosses Westbourne Terrace. Passing a souvenir stall (left) go left on to the towpath, walk under the bridge passing the former Grand Junction Canal Companies toll house (left), now a British Waterways Canal Office. The 147-mile journey now begins amid the moorings of some very elegant craft then passes the Victorian church of St Mary Magdalene (left) with blocks of flats (right).

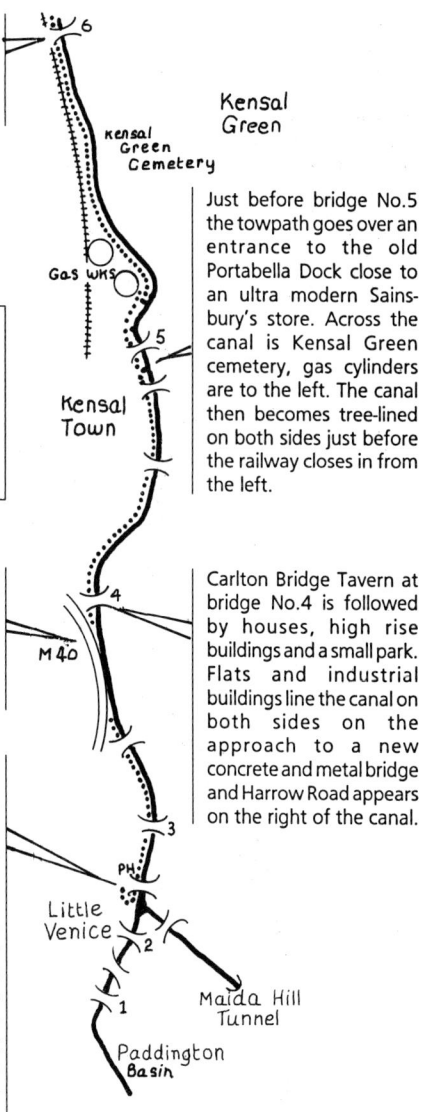

Just before bridge No.5 the towpath goes over an entrance to the old Portabella Dock close to an ultra modern Sainsbury's store. Across the canal is Kensal Green cemetery, gas cylinders are to the left. The canal then becomes tree-lined on both sides just before the railway closes in from the left.

Carlton Bridge Tavern at bridge No.4 is followed by houses, high rise buildings and a small park. Flats and industrial buildings line the canal on both sides on the approach to a new concrete and metal bridge and Harrow Road appears on the right of the canal.

THE GRAND UNION CANAL WALK

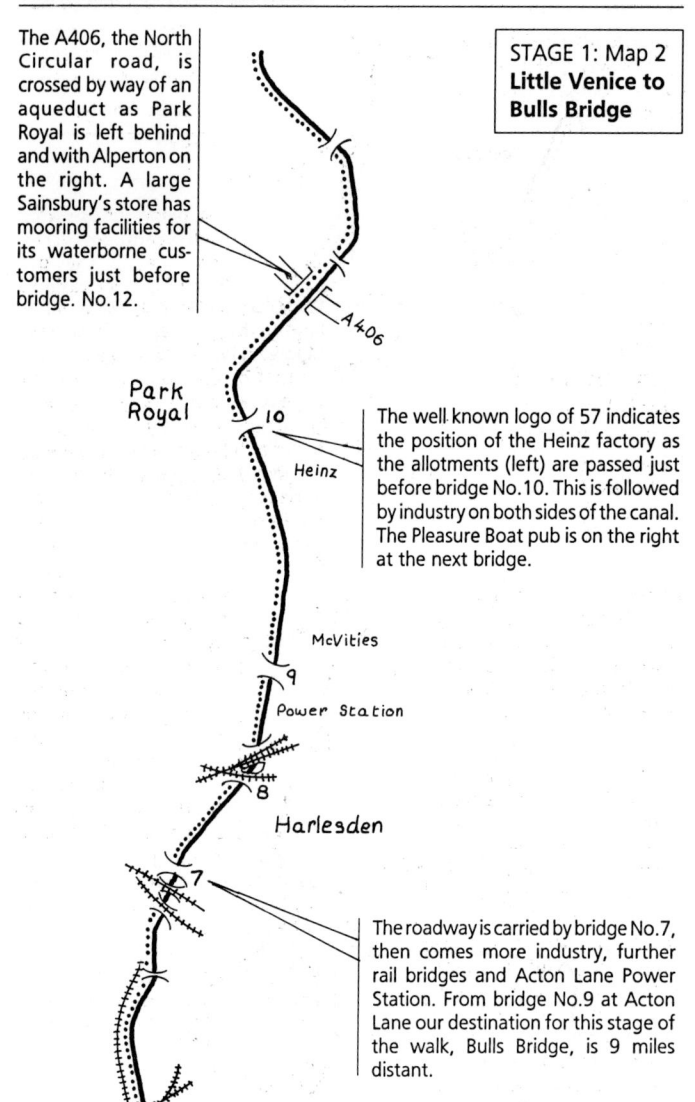

STAGE 1: Map 2
Little Venice to Bulls Bridge

The A406, the North Circular road, is crossed by way of an aqueduct as Park Royal is left behind and with Alperton on the right. A large Sainsbury's store has mooring facilities for its waterborne customers just before bridge. No.12.

Park Royal

Heinz

The well known logo of 57 indicates the position of the Heinz factory as the allotments (left) are passed just before bridge No.10. This is followed by industry on both sides of the canal. The Pleasure Boat pub is on the right at the next bridge.

McVities

Power Station

Harlesden

The roadway is carried by bridge No.7, then comes more industry, further rail bridges and Acton Lane Power Station. From bridge No.9 at Acton Lane our destination for this stage of the walk, Bulls Bridge, is 9 miles distant.

20

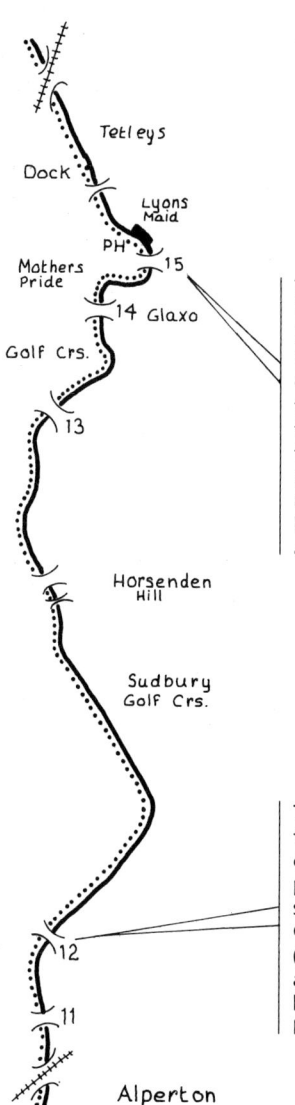

STAGE 1: Map 3
Little Venice to Bulls Bridge

The Glaxo works is close to bridge No.14, then comes Mothers pride before bridge No.15, followed by the Black Horse pub (left) situated opposite wide moorings. The towpath then passes the Hovis and Lyons factories before crossing the entrance to Lyons Dock by way of a footbridge. Soon comes Tetley's Tea (you can tell by the smell from the opposite canal bank) followed by old warehouses and factories to the left and right.

The towpath surface now deteriorates to gravel making progress less comfortable. Terraced houses are passed followed by hedges on both sides of the canal, then the Sudbury Golf Club reaches the water's edge (right). On the left are pleasant trees and for a while a little space beside a housing estate. Further to the right is Horsenden Hill.

THE GRAND UNION CANAL WALK

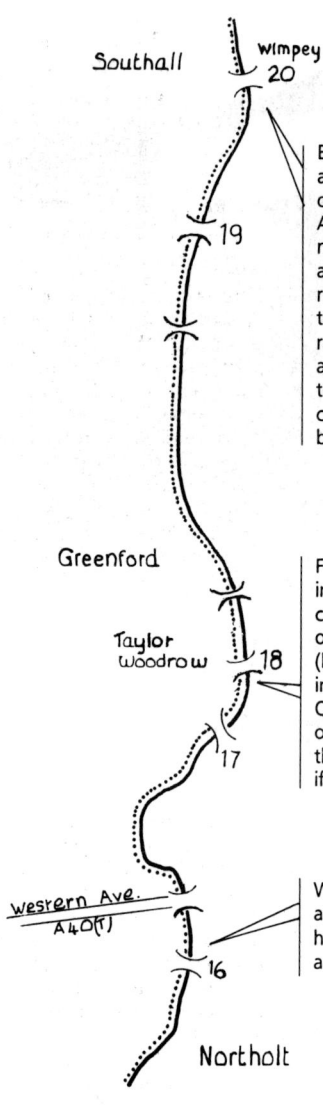

STAGE 1: Map 4
Little Venice to Bulls Bridge

Southall — Wimpey — 20

Bridge No.20 carries the busy A4020 road across the canal, beside which, to the left of the towpath, is the Hambrough Tavern. Across the canal is a B&Q DIY superstore next to EMI Music Service. Passing the allotments (left) the canal curves to the right while beyond a high wall beside the towpath are huge gas cylinders. After the railway bridge are factories, warehouses and a large mooring area (left) and then a toll house (right). Ahead, straddling the canal, is Bulls Bridge, to the left is Brentford but our route is to the right.

Greenford

Taylor Woodrow — 18 — 17

For a short distance after bridge No.18 industrial buildings are linked across the canal by two-storey bridges. A long stretch of parkland (right) follows with houses (left) and a sports ground (right). Passing industrial buildings on the left the West Quay Basin is across the canal and is overlooked by very modern buildings. On the towpath a couple of seats are provided if you need to take a break.

Western Ave. A40(T) — 16

Western Avenue is carried by bridge No.16 after which the canal zig-zags between houses before going into a shallow cutting and turning left under bridge No.18.

Northolt

STAGE 1 - LITTLE VENICE TO BULLS BRIDGE

The Old Toll House, Bulls Bridge

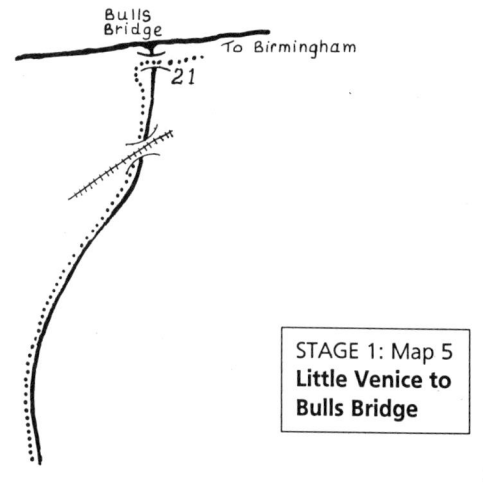

STAGE 1: Map 5
Little Venice to Bulls Bridge

STAGE 2:
Bulls Bridge to Harefield

PLACES AND POINTS OF INTEREST ALONG THE WAY

Bulls Bridge
Bulls Bridge is the junction of the Paddington Arm and the main branch of the Grand Union Canal. It was an important repair and maintenance centre for all the canal's commercial working life. No doubt it was all hustle and bustle then and a much grimier place than that used by the many house boats moored here today. Just left of the junction are moored many variations on the house boat design including one and two-storey varieties.

West Drayton
From Bulls Bridge junction our route continues through a canalside scene of 'industrial suburbia', a conglomeration of companies, scrap yards and wasteland. It is hard to imagine but over to the left of the towpath near bridge No.192, where West Drayton now stands, was the original village remodelled by the Paget family in 1550 at the same time as they built their fine Manor House. Some of the remaining walls of this red brick mansion surround the church of St Martin, parts of which date from the 1400s. Perhaps the most interesting thing about this church is the memorial to Captain Billingsley who was lost at sea with his crew of 800 men when, in 1782, the *Royal George* sank beneath the waves. The poem by William Cowper reads:

> *A land breeze shook the shrouds*
> *And she was overset*
> *Down went the Royal George*
> *With all her crew complete*

Yiewsley, Cowley Peachey and the Slough Arm
With Yiewsley on the right bank the canal swings north in a broad bend through the residential area of Cowley Peachey. On the main road stands the locally well known inn, the Paddington Packet Boat,

named after the popular pleasure boat that plied up and down the canal between Uxbridge and Paddington until almost 150 years ago.

On the left bank is the canal arm to Slough which being only 112 years old is one of Britain's most 'modern' canals. It was constructed primarily to provide transport for the brick works and gravel diggings as the western extremities of the capital developed. Later the large craters left by this extraction were used as infill sites for London's rubbish and today these tippings of yesteryear, so close to the canal, provide an unusual bonus for the modern-day collector of bric-a-brac of a bygone age. This 5-mile stretch of canal is also a popular place for birdwatchers and anglers.

Uxbridge

The canal and the River Colne flow side by side through Uxbridge which today is a combination of streets still containing half-timbered buildings, Georgian houses and modern shopping centres. In the past the town's prosperity came from the Colne, for it was a milling town but not always a quiet one as many millers belonged to the Society of Friends and locally there was a history of religious unrest. Three people were burned at the stake in 1555 in what is now Windson Street which was known previously as Lynch Green. In 1630 riots broke out in the town as people protested at the tolls being extracted by the Countess of Derby who was Lady of the Manor.

Possibly the most famous building in Uxbridge is the well preserved old inn known as The Crown which was once the grand home of Sir John Bennet. It was here in 1645 that representatives from both sides in the English Civil War met for the Treaty of Uxbridge in an effort to try to end the conflict. Unfortunately their problems were not solved and it was not until after the bloody battle at Naseby in Northamptonshire, four months later, that the war finally ended.

THE GRAND UNION CANAL WALK

Approaching Denham Deep Lock, No 87

STAGE 2 - BULLS BRIDGE TO HAREFIELD

THE GRAND UNION CANAL WALK

STAGE 2:
Bulls Bridge to Harefield
Map: Landranger 176
Start: GR. SU 106 792
Distance: 8¼ miles

A motor car scrap yard lies along the left of the canal for almost ¼ mile as the railway draws closer. New factory units can be seen to the right just before bridge No.193.

Beyond the white bridge No.197 the towpath can be quite muddy as it continues with a high fence (right) and the large ARC (Amey Roadstone) site (left). The next bridge carries the road high above the canal. Further on, the old bridge No.195 is followed by a modern concrete bridge at Ironbridge Road North. Soon on the left the canal passes a series of industrial complexes surrounded by rusting junk. Beyond the towpath a landscaped area is dotted with young trees.

For a while the sides of the canal become wooded while it passes between factories and under the fairly new brick-built bridge No.199. Scrubby wasteland follows on the right with trees on the left while buddleia bushes sprout colourfully from the edge of an old wharf.

Turn right and cross bridge No.21 (Bulls Bridge), a sign on the towpath indicating that Birmingham is straight ahead. Behind is a mooring with single and two-storey houseboats of various designs. On the left are rotting metal warehouses while ahead is a new road bridge and the huge Nestlé's factory (left). After the railway bridge is bridge No.200 before which the towpath crosses a footbridge spanning a disused canal junction amid high-rise buildings.

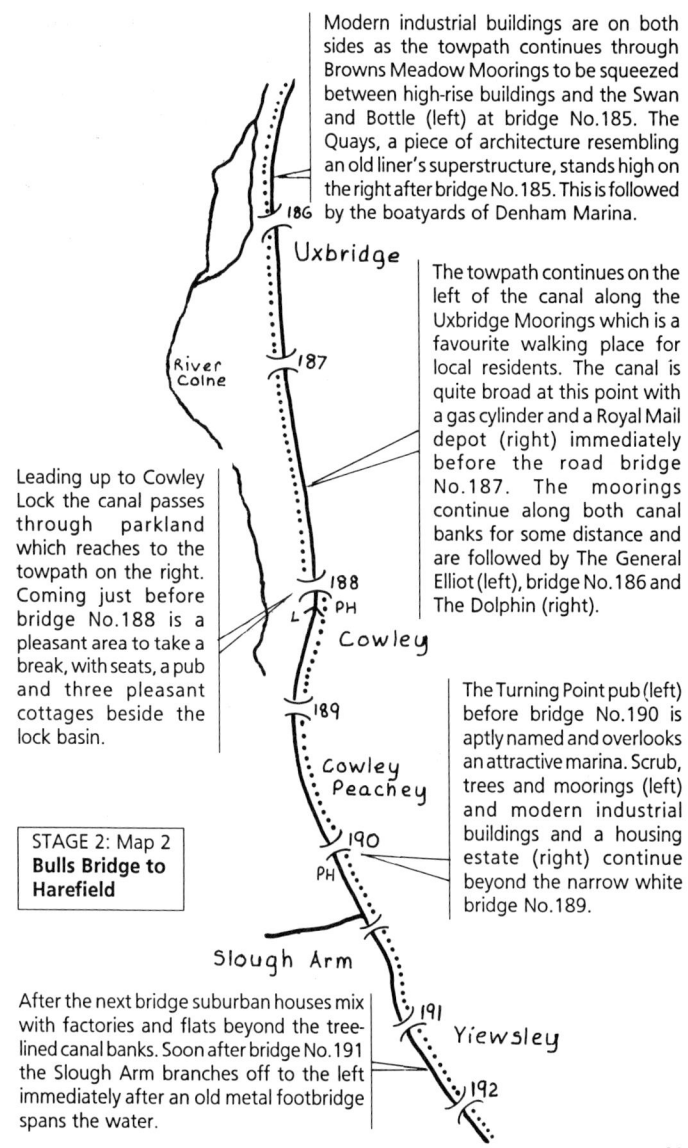

STAGE 2 - BULLS BRIDGE TO HAREFIELD

Modern industrial buildings are on both sides as the towpath continues through Browns Meadow Moorings to be squeezed between high-rise buildings and the Swan and Bottle (left) at bridge No.185. The Quays, a piece of architecture resembling an old liner's superstructure, stands high on the right after bridge No.185. This is followed by the boatyards of Denham Marina.

The towpath continues on the left of the canal along the Uxbridge Moorings which is a favourite walking place for local residents. The canal is quite broad at this point with a gas cylinder and a Royal Mail depot (right) immediately before the road bridge No.187. The moorings continue along both canal banks for some distance and are followed by The General Elliot (left), bridge No.186 and The Dolphin (right).

Leading up to Cowley Lock the canal passes through parkland which reaches to the towpath on the right. Coming just before bridge No.188 is a pleasant area to take a break, with seats, a pub and three pleasant cottages beside the lock basin.

STAGE 2: Map 2
Bulls Bridge to Harefield

The Turning Point pub (left) before bridge No.190 is aptly named and overlooks an attractive marina. Scrub, trees and moorings (left) and modern industrial buildings and a housing estate (right) continue beyond the narrow white bridge No.189.

After the next bridge suburban houses mix with factories and flats beyond the tree-lined canal banks. Soon after bridge No.191 the Slough Arm branches off to the left immediately after an old metal footbridge spans the water.

THE GRAND UNION CANAL WALK

STAGE 2: Map 3
Bulls Bridge to Harefield

The canal continues, broad and straight between dense woodland, under the black and white footbridge and between the high, graceful, multi-arched, brick viaduct that carries the railway east to west. Eventually the canal flows between several lakes. Harefield Marina is on the right just before bridge No.180, close to which stands The Horse and Barge.

Set amid grassy banks and surrounded by the woodland of Denham Country Park, Denham Deep Lock is a popular place. Refreshments are on sale at the white cottage.

Crossing over bridge No.184 the towpath continues along the right bank where, beside the lock with its smart-looking cottage, seats are provided. Across the canal stands the King William flour mill near an old canal arm and attractive modern houses are surrounded by their well-tended gardens. Sports fields now border the towpath and across the canal are residential areas. A tributary of the River Colne joins the canal just before it goes under the Oxford Road. Between the small, white bridge No.183 and the Denham Deep Lock there is a towpath on both of the canal banks.

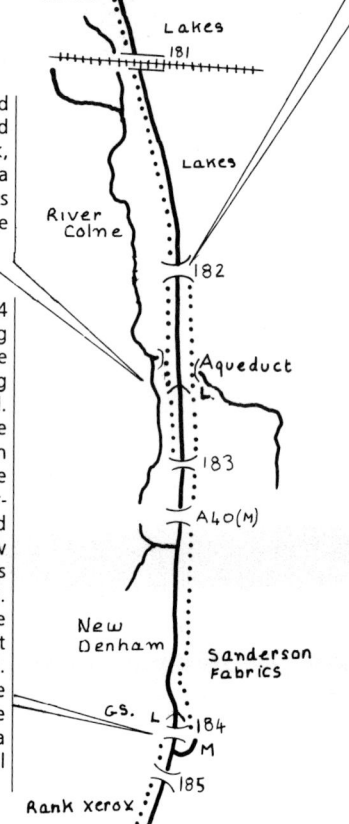

30

STAGE 2 - BULLS BRIDGE TO HAREFIELD

The Quay's at Denham, as seen from bridge 184

STAGE 3:
Harefield Marina to Apsley

PLACES AND POINTS OF INTEREST ALONG THE WAY

Harefield

For the next few miles the canal passes between a series of lakes, the result of flooding old gravel pits, while those still operating commercially are eaten away by huge clattering cranes. Just before South Harefield at bridge No.180 is the marina with a shop, toilet and telephone facilities. In Harefield itself the half-timbered inn The King's Arms sits at the edge of the village green while almshouses, dating from Elizabethan times, can be found nearby. Perhaps the most interesting place hereabouts is Black Jack's Lock close by the old corn mill. It is said that many years ago when boatmen would slip through the locks at night in order to avoid paying the dues, a large black African who became known as Black Jack, was employed to enforce the rules. This he seemed to do with some success until he was murdered by an infuriated boatman who had been harassed too much and since then Black Jack is said to haunt the locks.

Jordans Village

At Copper Mill Lock just past bridge No.177 there is not a lot to see but before we progress further north it is worth mentioning that at this point on the canal we are barely 4 miles east of the village of Jordans. This village has a connection, via the Society of Friends, with Uxbridge through which we passed a few miles back.

During the 17th century a group of Quakers farmed at William Russell's farm Old Jordans and today's village, built as recently as 1919, is derived from that name. The village continued to develop until 1923 by which time numerous cottages and houses had been erected around a village green. These are now rented out on monthly tenancies. The original farm of Old Jordans now belongs to the same organisation, the Society of Friends, and has become a guesthouse while the now famous barn, reputedly built from the timbers of the *Mayflower*, is used for large gatherings and concerts.

Close to the barn and beside the road to Beaconsfield is the original Friends Meeting House built during the reign of James II when he had issued his Declaration of Indulgence which aimed to give freedom of worship not only for Catholics but also for the Quakers. The house was built on a slope thus enabling it to function as a meeting place with accommodation in its single-storey end for a raised dais for the elders. At its two-storey end, where the ground slopes away, the living accommodation for the caretaker was incorporated. A very practical piece of architectural design for the period.

A debt of £16,000, a lot of money in those days, was owed to the father of William Penn by Charles II but instead of repayment in cash the king gave a large piece of land, Pennsylvania as it is today, in discharge and this was passed by his father to William Penn. A code of high-minded principles under which this part of the 'New World' should be run was laid down by Penn although they were far from being practical. The state prospered and immigrants swelled the number of those who believed in Penn's methods of government. Today he is remembered as the founder of the state of Pennsylvania and the city of Philadelphia and is buried in the small graveyard in front of the Friends Meeting House.

Rickmansworth

Rickmansworth was established at the confluence of three rivers, the Chess, the Gade and the Colne. At the time of Domesday it was called Rychemreworde but later when Henry VIII granted a charter it was known as Rykemeresworth which aptly described the place as 'land between the rivers'.

The local landowning family, the Carey's, are remembered in the church not least of all as on the death of Elizabeth I, Robert Carey travelled north to inform James VI of Scotland that he had just become also King of England.

The reader will no doubt recall the connection with the early Quakers at Uxbridge and Jordans during Stage 2 of our walk; another connection is at Rickmansworth. William Penn and his wife were married in 1672 and for five years lived at Basing House, now the council office, just to the north of the church, with the Bury, the priory and the old vicarage close by.

Referred to as the most splendid 18th-century mansion in Hertfordshire, Moore Park is situated about a mile away and is now

THE GRAND UNION CANAL WALK

Black Jack's Lock

STAGE 3 - HAREFIELD MARINA TO APSLEY

a prestigious clubhouse for a golf club. It was constructed of Portland stone during 1725-27 by Sir James Thornhill. The hallway is two storeys high and has a balcony, marble doorways, statues and large Venetian paintings on the walls and ceilings. The grounds were landscaped by Capability Brown in 1758.

Rickmansworth never expanded at the same rate as nearby Watford but in 1887 the Metropolitan Railway stretched out from London and by the late 1920s the town had lost its residential image. People working in the city liked the idea of living on the edge of the Chilterns, just as their children do today. Thus Rickmansworth is very much part of a modern development with just a little of the past left intact.

Croxley Mills and the Parks of Cassiobury, Grove and Langley Bury

Just to the right after the lock at bridge No.170 is the former site of Dickinson's Croxley Mills. For 150 years, right up until 1970, the canal narrowboats transported coal for the production of paper at Croxley Mills.

Just to the north after bridge No.168 is Cassiobury Park, a fine example of a water park on the very edge of busy Watford. Here the canal glides through a series of parks with woodland covering its banks where wildlife is very much in evidence, and the west Hertfordshire Golf Course is over to the left.

Proceeding northwards you come to Grove Park, at one time the home of the Earls of Clarendon and where the old Grove Mill has been converted into modern apartments with an interesting collection of old machinery spread affectionately across the lawns.

Finally comes Langley Bury where the King's Lodge restaurant was originally built as a hunting lodge for Charles II in 1642.

The Langleys

Hunton Bridge is a quiet village set beside the canal and just south of Kings Langley where a palace was built by Henry III. Little remains of the palace except for a 13th-century wine cellar which was unearthed when the foundations of the Rudolph Steiner school were being dug out in 1970. The remains of a friary, dating from the early 1300s, can still be seen and from here the body of Edmund of Langley, the first Duke of York, who was born at the palace in 1341, was interred before being placed in All Saints church after the Dissolution.

Today the main street is very busy but it still retains some of its interesting character of times past. The Saracen's Head dates in part from the 17th century and is neighbour to various flint and red brick houses.

Described by some people as a bit of Disneyland, the half-timbered and thatched, purpose-built Ovaltine Egg Farm is perhaps the most unusual building in Abbots Langley. It was built in 1931 and has now been converted into up-market houses. There is little left of the old village, most of it having been swallowed up by suburban development, but a tablet in the church of St Lawrence reminds us of the village's most famous son, Nicholas Breakspear. Nicholas was born in the hamlet of Bedmond during the 11th century. His father Robert became a monk at St Albans Abbey and when Nicholas tried to follow in his father's footsteps the Abbot refused him. Later he travelled to Avignon, France, and entered the Abbey of St Rufus, eventually becoming the Abbot. The Pope got to hear of his dedication and hard work and made him a cardinal, sending him to Scandinavia as a missionary. In 1154 Pope Anastasius died and Nicholas was elected to become his successor; as such he became Pope Adrian IV, the only English pope.

The kingfisher, frequently seen along this stretch of the canal

THE GRAND UNION CANAL WALK

Lynsters Lake is to the left of the towpath, and cottages, houses and bungalows now line each side of the canal. The Maple Cross Sewerage Works (left) is unmistakable and is followed by the Springwell Reedbed Nature Reserve. A group of houses (right) is situated before the white bridge at Springwell Locks.

STAGE 3:
Harefield Marina to Apsley
Map: Landranger 176
Start: GR. SU 050 887
Distance: 12½ miles

A small estate of modern houses, with their own quays, soon appears on the right of the canal while Fishery Cottage, next to the towpath, is a more traditional dwelling. The Fisheries Inn is beside the towpath at bridge No.177. Across the canal from Copper Mill Lock the old foundry buildings are undergoing conversion to private apartments.

Approaching bridge No.178, white with a brick parapet, the land rises quite steeply up to the right where the house at the top of the field commands excellent views over the canal and the lakes beyond. On the other side of the bridge is Black Jack's Lock, with the old mill and restaurant beside the towpath, after which the canal continues through an area of picturesque trees. From here right up to Batchworth there are no less than seven footbridges that take the towpath over small rivers and culverts linking the canal to the vast area of lakes (left), the first of which is encountered shortly after Black Jack's Lock.

After bridge No.180 and the Widewater Lock the towpath is on the left of the canal. There are industrial and office buildings, a housing estate and a pillbox, left over from the Second World War, on the right of the canal. After the next bridge there are good views to the left across the Harefield Flashes and a fine selection of trees dipping down into the water on the canal's right bank, making a colourful show during late summer and autumn.

38

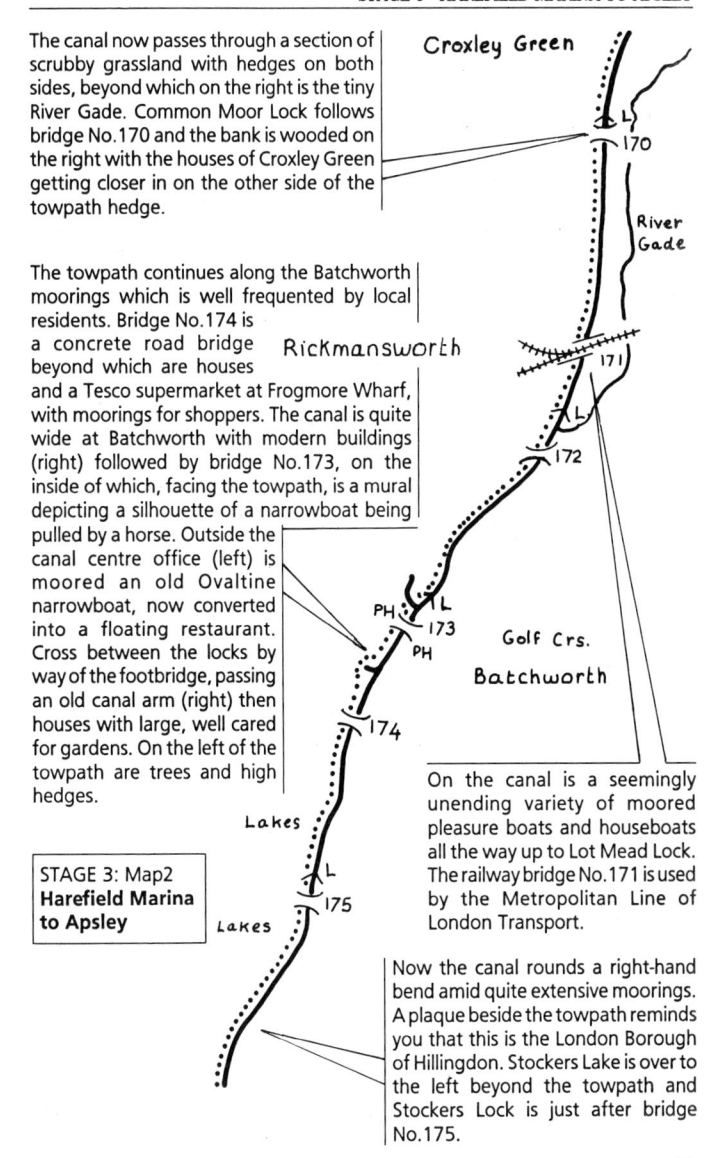

STAGE 3 - HAREFIELD MARINA TO APSLEY

The canal now passes through a section of scrubby grassland with hedges on both sides, beyond which on the right is the tiny River Gade. Common Moor Lock follows bridge No.170 and the bank is wooded on the right with the houses of Croxley Green getting closer in on the other side of the towpath hedge.

The towpath continues along the Batchworth moorings which is well frequented by local residents. Bridge No.174 is a concrete road bridge beyond which are houses and a Tesco supermarket at Frogmore Wharf, with moorings for shoppers. The canal is quite wide at Batchworth with modern buildings (right) followed by bridge No.173, on the inside of which, facing the towpath, is a mural depicting a silhouette of a narrowboat being pulled by a horse. Outside the canal centre office (left) is moored an old Ovaltine narrowboat, now converted into a floating restaurant. Cross between the locks by way of the footbridge, passing an old canal arm (right) then houses with large, well cared for gardens. On the left of the towpath are trees and high hedges.

STAGE 3: Map2
Harefield Marina to Apsley

On the canal is a seemingly unending variety of moored pleasure boats and houseboats all the way up to Lot Mead Lock. The railway bridge No.171 is used by the Metropolitan Line of London Transport.

Now the canal rounds a right-hand bend amid quite extensive moorings. A plaque beside the towpath reminds you that this is the London Borough of Hillingdon. Stockers Lake is over to the left beyond the towpath and Stockers Lock is just after bridge No.175.

39

THE GRAND UNION CANAL WALK

Pass beneath two noisy road bridges then up to the attractive Hunton Bridge Locks close to the busy A41. Here boats are moored on both sides of the canal. At bridge No.162 is The King's head pub (right).

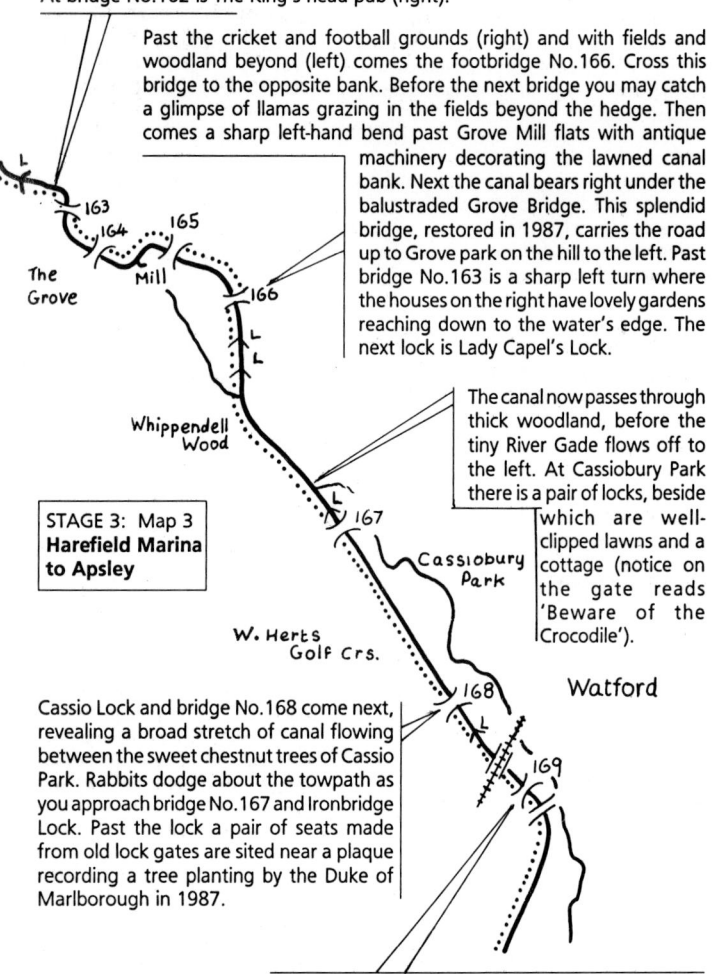

Past the cricket and football grounds (right) and with fields and woodland beyond (left) comes the footbridge No.166. Cross this bridge to the opposite bank. Before the next bridge you may catch a glimpse of llamas grazing in the fields beyond the hedge. Then comes a sharp left-hand bend past Grove Mill flats with antique machinery decorating the lawned canal bank. Next the canal bears right under the balustraded Grove Bridge. This splendid bridge, restored in 1987, carries the road up to Grove park on the hill to the left. Past bridge No.163 is a sharp left turn where the houses on the right have lovely gardens reaching down to the water's edge. The next lock is Lady Capel's Lock.

The canal now passes through thick woodland, before the tiny River Gade flows off to the left. At Cassiobury Park there is a pair of locks, beside which are well-clipped lawns and a cottage (notice on the gate reads 'Beware of the Crocodile').

STAGE 3: Map 3
Harefield Marina to Apsley

Cassio Lock and bridge No.168 come next, revealing a broad stretch of canal flowing between the sweet chestnut trees of Cassio Park. Rabbits dodge about the towpath as you approach bridge No.167 and Ironbridge Lock. Past the lock a pair of seats made from old lock gates are sited near a plaque recording a tree planting by the Duke of Marlborough in 1987.

As the towpath nears Watford, over to the right, it passes beneath four bridges carrying road and rail. One bridge is dated 1921. The Bridgewater Basin and Marina are to the right before the fourth of these bridges.

STAGE 3 - HAREFIELD MARINA TO APSLEY

The sweet smell of 'bedtime' drinks wafts across the canal from the Ovaltine works while on the left an ornamental lake with a galleon and static missiles is visible from the towpath. At bridge No.158 cross the canal to the other bank. Pass the lock and bridge No.157. After a slight bend the canal broadens considerably. There are lakes (right) and fields and a main road (left).

Kings Langley

To the right of the towpath is the Rickmansworth Water Works with the railway beyond it. After Home Park Farm Lock the towpath goes under the M25 motorway amid an area of farmland. Bridge No.159 is a footbridge, then comes a road bridge and Home Park Mill Lock with its attendant cottage (right).

Ovaltine Wks.

Mill

Rly. Station

M25

Abbots Langley

Hunton Bridge

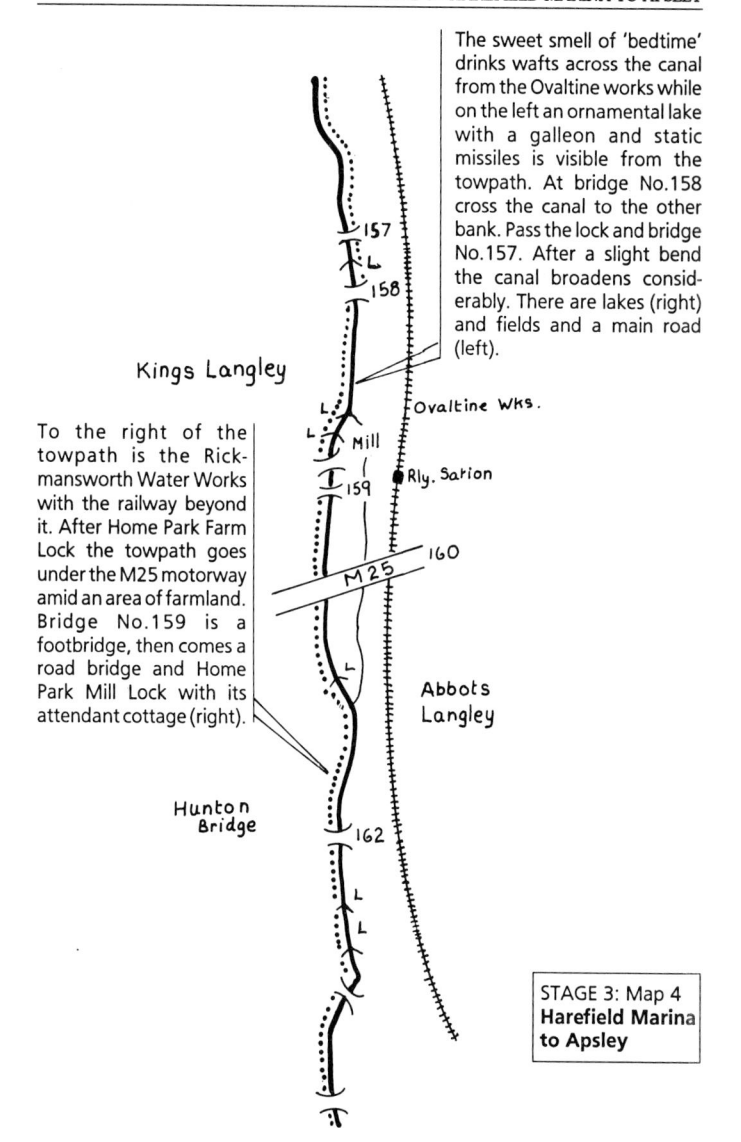

STAGE 3: Map 4
Harefield Marina to Apsley

THE GRAND UNION CANAL WALK

> STAGE 3: Map 5
> **Harefield Marina to Apsley**

Under the high arched railway bridge the canal bends left through suburban industry. Cross to the left at the next bridge, pass Nash Mills Lock then the modern buildings of Dickensons, the paper manufacturers (left). Use the small white footbridge to cross the canal again, pass Apsley Mill Moorings with the lock and then the large Sainsbury's store (left)

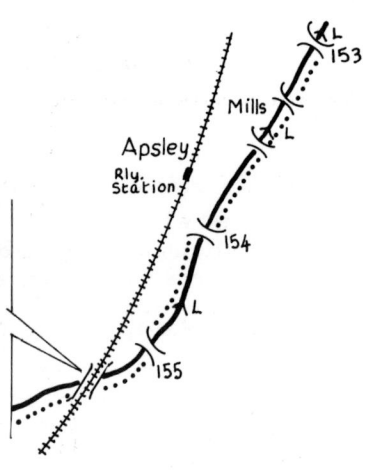

STAGE 4:
Apsley to Bulbourne

PLACES AND POINTS OF INTEREST ALONG THE WAY

Hemel Hempstead

Today Hemel Hempstead is regarded by many as being synonymous with the name of Kodak but before the days of photography the town had grown up close to its Norman church, with its High Street running along a low ridge above the River Gade.

The church of St Mary is claimed to be the finest Norman church in Hertfordshire. Constructed of flint and brick it took 40 years to complete, the building having started in 1140. The most significant feature of the church is the tall spire rising to almost 200ft, set atop its tall central tower.

Hemel Hempstead's original town hall built in 1851 and situated in the High Street has been preserved in spite of the threat of demolition when the new town hall was built. Evidence of the past can be seen on many of the buildings where dates of the early 1700s are to be found above their drainpipes. A cast iron pump with a lamp built by John Cranstone in 1848 is situated at the end of the High Street.

The Paston Cooper family have resided in the area for many years and Sir Astley Paston Cooper, who lived at Gadebridge Park, was sergeant-surgeon to Queen Victoria, William IV and before that to George IV.

Boxmoor and Bourne End

Until the development of the canal and later the building of the railway, Boxmoor was a small hamlet with common grazing land on the local marshland through which the canal now passes. This marshland has always been known as the 'moor' and some of the older houses in the High Street still display the old Rights of Pasture plaques, a right which still exists to graze poultry and cattle on this common land.

A very small part of the 'moor' marked by two white stones, became the final resting place for Robert Snooks, the local highwayman who was hung nearby. A local tale goes that whilst being transported to his hanging place he noticed that the villagers were hurrying about and there was a certain air of excitement. He enquired as to what was going on and when informed, by one of them who didn't recognise him, that they were off to see a hanging he is said to have replied "Until I get there nothing can happen".

As though to indicate some independence from Hemel Hempstead, to which it has now become attached and nearly overwhelmed by modern development, Boxmoor still retains its separate church of 1874 by Norman Shaw.

L. Rose & Co, the well known manufacturers of lime juice, were for many years established at Boxmoor and until 1980 the raw pulp for their fruit juices was delivered to their canalside wharfs by narrowboat.

Barely a couple of miles along the towpath is Bourne End, a spot of a place on the former Roman road, Akemann Street, now the busy A41. Here, where a small stream forms the boundary with Buckinghamshire and joins the River Bulbourne, George Gilbert Scott, famous for designing the Midland Grand Hotel at St Pancras Station in London, built the church of St John in 1854. The church sits amongst the attractive evergreens of this lush valley which is but a small cleft in the Chilterns and is accompanied by a sprinkle of cottages alongside the farm tracks. An old mill near the lock has in recent years now been converted to a restaurant; formerly the Watermill Hotel it is now the Moat House.

Berkhamstead

The crown of England was offered to William the Conqueror by the defeated Saxon nobles at Berkhamstead. Some time after this William's half brother Robert, Earl of Mortain, built a motte and bailey just north of the river. Sadly not much of it is left today, apart from the earthworks which are still recognisable, and fragments of the curtain wall stand gauntly around the spacious lawns of the former bailey. As the Duke of Cornwall, the Black Prince resided here and at one time King John of France was imprisoned at Berkhamstead Castle.

A further connection with the past is through the chief cook to Charles II who, when he died, left money in his will for almshouses to be built. They were to consist of 12 rooms and were to accommodate six widows. They still stand near the main road junction on the High Street.

At the top of Castle Street is the church of St Peter, one of the largest churches in Hertfordshire. The church contains many memorials, notably the east window which is a memorial to the poet William Cowper. His father was the rector at St Peter's when William was born in 1731 and he was brought up in the rectory. He is perhaps best remembered for his poem *John Gilpin*. Just to the south of the church is the well restored 16th-century Incent House.

Berkhamstead, with numerous old inns and places to eat, is an interesting town in which to spend a while. It bustles with activity and in the main is a pleasant blend of architecture of the last two centuries mixed with those of more recent times.

Northchurch

At its peak Northchurch was more important than Berkhamstead and was known as Berkhamstead St Mary. Today, although it is almost a complete continuation of its much larger neighbour, Northchurch is to its residents an individual and separate village. To the south lies the ancient Grimms Ditch passing through gently undulating land dotted with coppice and woodland, while to the north are large areas of open common below Ashridge.

Considerable development has taken place in the village during recent years but it still retains its connections with times past. If you walk in the graveyard of the church, St Mary's, you may come across the stone which marks the grave of 'Peter the Wild Boy 1785'. The stone indicates the resting place of what in those days was an unfortunate freak; for Peter was found in a forest near Hanover in Germany in 1725. He walked on all fours and ate grass as sustenance. His presence came to the notice of George I and no doubt for his novelty value Peter was duly persuaded to come to England. Eventually he was placed in the care of a group of farmers at Northchurch where he survived until his death in 1785.

Cowroast

Cowroast used to be the spot where the cattle drovers of old took a break and stopped for the night during their journey to London. Over a period of time Cow Rest became known as Cowroast, thus giving quite the wrong impression. There is little of importance here, the village consisting of a few dwellings, a couple of good pubs and a marina with a small shop. The picturesque Cowroast lock is almost 400ft above the River Thames. We are now therefore quite high up considering that we are walking beside a canal.

Aldbury

About a mile east of bridge No.135 is the picturesque village of Aldbury sitting amidst the downs of the nearby common land. The village's main street with its 16th and 17th-century half-timbered cottages opens out onto a small green complete with stocks, whipping post and an eye-catching pond. Close to the Chantry cottages and just across from the stocks is an unusual building in brick which was the former bakehouse and washhouse, a combination quite unique to this village.

A monument to the so-called 'father of inland navigation', Francis, the third Duke of Bridgewater, is situated on Aldbury Common. The 200ft high, rather austere-looking Doric column with an urn on its top stands in a clearing near the edge of the common and is approached through a tree-lined avenue of over a mile in length. The monument has 172 steps leading to a viewing platform from where fine views across the vale of Aylesbury can be seen.

Tring

About $1^1/_2$ miles to the east of the canal is the centre of Tring. Known at the time of Domesday as Trerung it was developed at the junction of Akeman Street with the Icknield Way. It remained a country place, virtually passed by and isolated until the building of the canal suddenly offered it the opportunity to develop along with other places on the route. This it seems to have done with no great enthusiasm for there is little of any note here.

STAGE 4 - APSLEY TO BULBOURNE

The locks at Cowroast

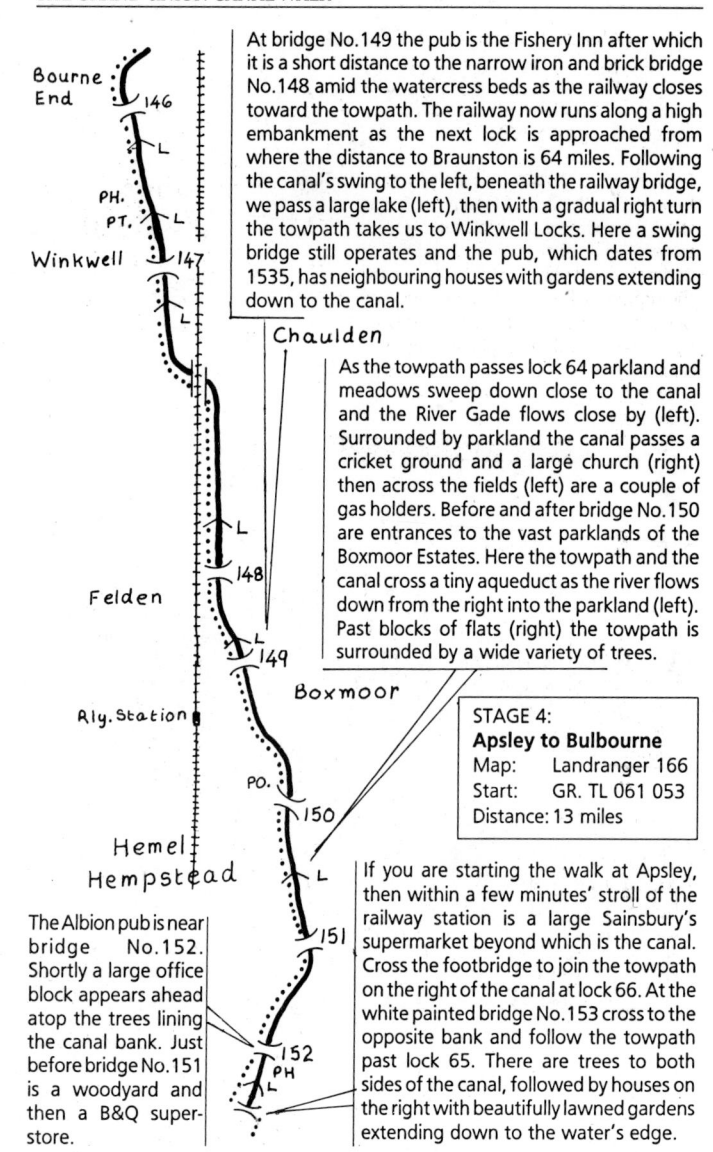

THE GRAND UNION CANAL WALK

At bridge No.149 the pub is the Fishery Inn after which it is a short distance to the narrow iron and brick bridge No.148 amid the watercress beds as the railway closes toward the towpath. The railway now runs along a high embankment as the next lock is approached from where the distance to Braunston is 64 miles. Following the canal's swing to the left, beneath the railway bridge, we pass a large lake (left), then with a gradual right turn the towpath takes us to Winkwell Locks. Here a swing bridge still operates and the pub, which dates from 1535, has neighbouring houses with gardens extending down to the canal.

As the towpath passes lock 64 parkland and meadows sweep down close to the canal and the River Gade flows close by (left). Surrounded by parkland the canal passes a cricket ground and a large church (right) then across the fields (left) are a couple of gas holders. Before and after bridge No.150 are entrances to the vast parklands of the Boxmoor Estates. Here the towpath and the canal cross a tiny aqueduct as the river flows down from the right into the parkland (left). Past blocks of flats (right) the towpath is surrounded by a wide variety of trees.

STAGE 4:
Apsley to Bulbourne
Map: Landranger 166
Start: GR. TL 061 053
Distance: 13 miles

If you are starting the walk at Apsley, then within a few minutes' stroll of the railway station is a large Sainsbury's supermarket beyond which is the canal. Cross the footbridge to join the towpath on the right of the canal at lock 66. At the white painted bridge No.153 cross to the opposite bank and follow the towpath past lock 65. There are trees to both sides of the canal, followed by houses on the right with beautifully lawned gardens extending down to the water's edge.

The Albion pub is near bridge No.152. Shortly a large office block appears ahead atop the trees lining the canal bank. Just before bridge No.151 is a woodyard and then a B&Q superstore.

48

STAGE 4 - APSLEY TO BULBOURNE

At Northchurch the towpath passes a collection of town houses and flats (left) and factory units (right). The canal continues to climb through locks up towards bridge No.139.

Cross bridge No.141 and follow the towpath on the left of the canal. For a short distance the towpath follows the edge of a small area of parkland with Berkhamstead railway station across to the right and, beyond it, the castle. Go beneath the black and red painted cast iron bridge with the old warehouse buildings (right). The canal then passes through parkland and the football club is to the right.

As the canal passes through the town it climbs up through a further three locks. On the right is the Rising Sun then The Boat followed by a row of terraced houses. On the opposite side is Bridgewater Boats at Castle Wharf, then at the timber yard, close by bridge No.141, stands a huge totem pole. The Crystal Palace (right) stands next to the railway.

Cross the canal by way of bridge No.143 and follow the towpath on the right of the canal, bringing the railway even closer. Houses and flats are across the canal followed by various industrial establishments.

STAGE 4: Map 2
Apsley to Bulbourne

At Bourne End there are three locks 58, 57 and 56 with the unfortunate names of Sewerage, Bottomside and Topside Locks. Bridge No.144 is just before the third one, where immediately the suburbs of Berkhamstead are encountered.

49

THE GRAND UNION CANAL WALK

**STAGE 4: Map 3
Apsley to Bulbourne**

Bulbourne
PH 133
134
Tring Summit
Cowroast
135
136
M
L
137
L
L
138
Dudswell
L
139
Rly. Station

Just after bridge No.136 are two large brick-built warehouses on top of a high quay (left). The canal then enters a deep cutting overhung with trees. This section of the canal is known as the Tring Summit. The canal turns gradually right, left and right again before straightening out for about one mile just before Bulbourne is reached. Midway along this stretch is the high, ivy-clad bridge No.134; cross this to follow the towpath on the left of the canal to Bulbourne and bridge No.133.

The attractive lock at Cowroast has a busy wharf and an extensive marina (right). Cross the footbridge over the marina entrance and continue ahead through Tring Summit Moorings. Soon the canal widens out with trees right down to the water's edge on the left and a high hedge beside the towpath.

At Dudswell cross bridge No.138 and follow the towpath on the right of the canal passing locks 47 and 48. The trees to the left fail to stifle the traffic noise from the A41 and the railway rumbles past on the right.

Approaching bridge No.139 the houses (right) have a fine position overlooking the canal. After Bush Lock there are allotments (left) then a housing estate with waste ground and the railway beyond (right).

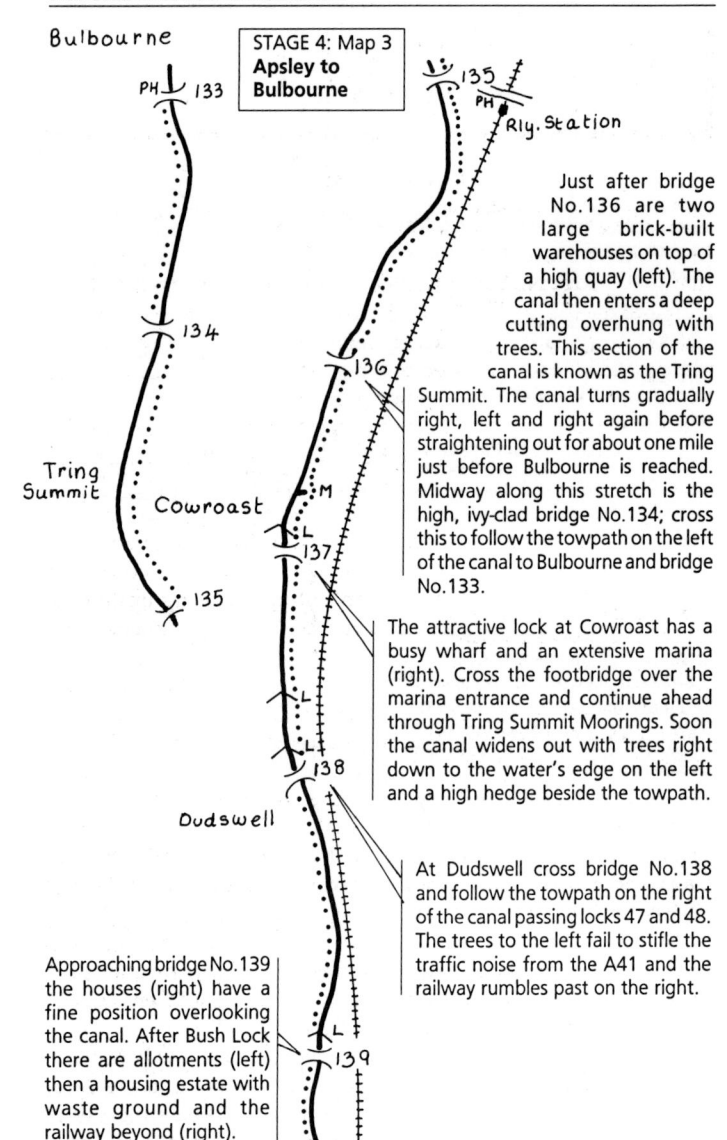

50

STAGE 5:
Bulbourne to Three Locks

PLACES AND POINTS OF INTEREST ALONG THE WAY

The Wendover Arm

Just after bridge No.133 comes the canal arm to Wendover with its own bridge No.1 crossing it at the T-junction. Its length of about 7 miles was originally intended as a feeder canal but in 1794 permission was granted for it to be used as a navigable commercial canal. Its water sources were three in number, Western Turville, Halton and Wendover, but it still proved to be unsatisfactory and was continually low on water. From the early 1800s and for almost 40 years a series of reservoirs were constructed locally to try to overcome the water shortage but the problem was never really solved. The canal therefore had a limited financial success and was finally abandoned as a commercial venture in 1904. Since then part has been restored and it is hoped that in the not too distant future, by using up-to-date engineering technology, the canal may be completely opened up.

Marsworth

Marsworth is rated as one of the most picturesque parts of the whole of the Grand Union Canal. The village is enclosed on three sides by the canal from bridge No.132 up to bridge No.129. Below bridge No.131 the canal's Aylesbury Arm turns off to the west.

Originally this canal was known as the Western Junction and it was intended that it would link up with the Wiltshire and Berkshire Canal and in so doing become a more direct route to the south-west of England by avoiding the capital city. Unfortunately the landowners and waterways owners who would be affected by this development protested so strongly that the idea of the canal to the west of Aylesbury was quashed and only the $6^{1}/_{2}$ mile length with its 16 locks was built. This was completed in 1815.

The Aylesbury branch was purposely made narrow in order to reduce the amount of water being used but even so the local reservoir at Wilstone was enlarged on two occasions in order to supply the new canal with badly needed water. Twenty years after this canal was opened Nestlés (in 1870 it was known as the Aylesbury Condensed Milk Company) established itself at Aylesbury, no doubt attracted in part by the presence of the new canal. Despite the development of the railways over the years the canal continued to carry building materials and coal to, and livestock and farm produce from Aylesbury until about 40 years ago, after which the commercial traffic on the waterway became sporadic. Things had deteriorated completely by the early 1970s and restoration work was commenced in 1973 by the newly formed Aylesbury Canal Society.

Ivinghoe
From Pitston Wharf the canal passes through three locks, Top, Lock, Seabrook Lock and Bottom Lock close to bridge No.123 at Ivinghoe Road. Close to the bridge is the former Brownlow Arms, now a private dwelling, and to the east is the high point of the downs, the Ivinghoe Beacon, which is about 760ft high. The gliders of the London Gliding Club can often be seen around its summit. Ivinghoe Beacon was an important fort during prehistoric times and over the years a number of Iron Age finds have been made close to it. It has been suggested that Sir Walter Scott probably took the name and modified it for the title of his famous novel *Ivanhoe*.

Pitstone and Cheddington
Pitstone consists primarily of residential areas for the nearby cement works. Clothed in heavy grey dust the buildings themselves stand out quite starkly on a flat plain with the distant Chiltern hills forming a backdrop. Insignificant in size by comparison is the old mill at Pitstone. Now owned by the National Trust and open during the summer months, it dates from 1627 and is said to be the oldest still standing in England.

Near bridge No.126 is the Pitstone Wharf with useful toilet facilities and a shop selling ice-cream, but for something stronger try the Duke of Wellington. Alternatively take to the road for a mile or so where, to the north-east, is Cheddington. Here you can choose between the Three Horseshoes or the Swan. Not far away is Mentmore House built by Joseph Paxton in 1854 for Baron Rothschild. Tours of this fine dwelling are held during the afternoon and the grounds are open daily.

STAGE 5 - BULBOURNE TO THREE LOCKS

Anglers at Bridge 126, near Cheddington

Leighton Buzzard and Linslade

Some people will recall the Great Train Robbery and its association with Linslade but well before that it had developed and become joined to nearby Leighton Buzzard. Both places were only separated by the canal and the River Ouzel running side by side at this point. Here there are numerous shops, eating places and pubs to choose from and in Leighton Buzzard a pleasant selection of architecture ranging from office blocks to brick and timber thatched cottages. In the market square the cross dates from the very beginning of the 15th century and the Golden Bells Inn is reputed to be older again. In North Street, Holly Lodge dates from the 1600s and close by are the old Wilkies Almshouses.

Quite a novelty of Leighton Buzzard is the narrow gauge railway which uses historic steam locomotives to haul train loads of visitors during the spring and summer through the town and out into the surrounding countryside.

Wildlife on Tring Reservoirs

STAGE 5 - BULBOURNE TO THREE LOCKS

> STAGE 5:
> **Bulbourne to Three Locks**
> Map: Landranger 165
> Start: GR. SU 933 137
> Distance: 9½ miles

Beyond bridge No.130 the canal passes between a tree-lined area for a while and right on the towpath is The Ship, not a pub but a black and white thatched shop. Past rolling hills (left) and farmland beyond the trees (right) you approach the tall chimneys of the Pitstone Cement Works, but it will take quite a bit of walking before we are past them. Past bridge No.129 you soon reach the next pair of locks, No.38 and Bottom Lock No.37.

Take the bridge over the Wendover Arm following the signpost reading Braunston 55 miles. Pass the Marsworth Flight of locks, the first of which is Marsworth Top Lock. From here the canal descends in a broad zig-zag with the Tring Reservoirs (left). As you approach the double-arched bridge No.132, with the White Lion pub beside it, the tall tower of Marsworth church is clearly visible (right). After a further ¼ mile of walking, cross to the Aylesbury Arm and pass the British Waterways office, walking through the yard and aiming as if you were going to cross the footbridge. Don't cross the footbridge; cross the stile ahead with the yellow marker indicating 'Circular Walk', then go down beyond the footbridge to join the towpath once more.

At bridge No.133 the Grand Junction pub is on the left and the Bulbourne workshop of British Waterways are across the canal from the towpath. Pass the barbecue area beside the towpath and in about ½ mile you reach the Wendover Arm of the canal at Bulbourne Junction.

THE GRAND UNION CANAL WALK

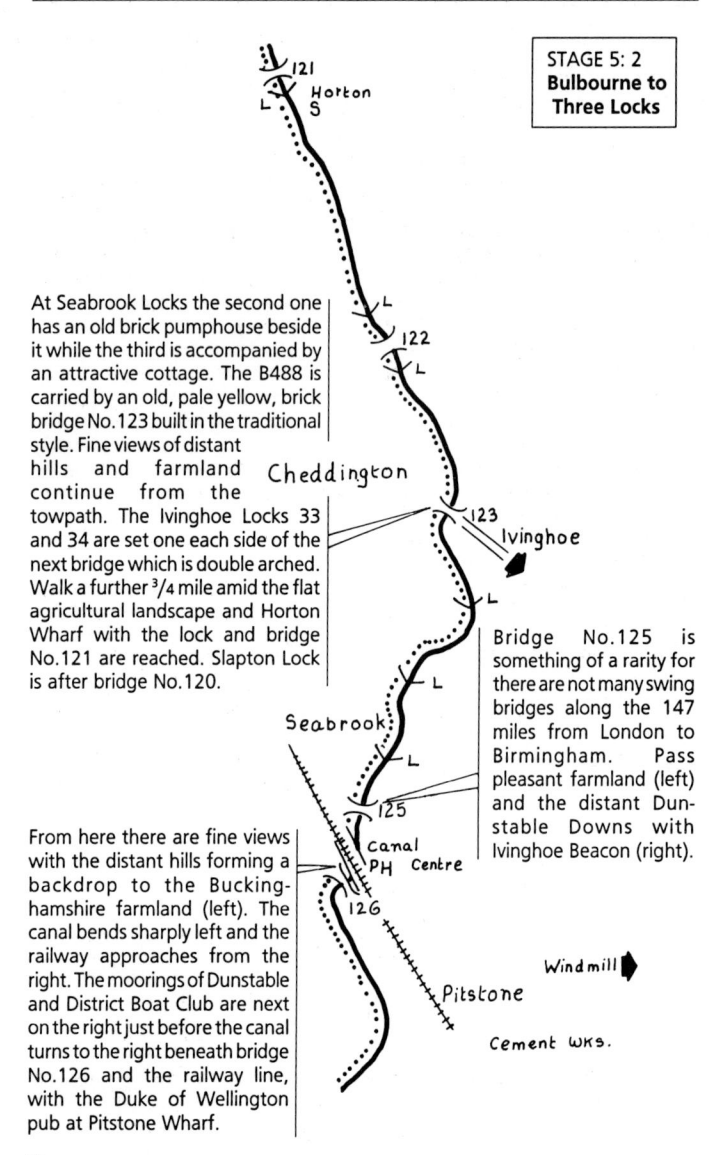

**STAGE 5: 2
Bulbourne to
Three Locks**

At Seabrook Locks the second one has an old brick pumphouse beside it while the third is accompanied by an attractive cottage. The B488 is carried by an old, pale yellow, brick bridge No.123 built in the traditional style. Fine views of distant hills and farmland continue from the towpath. The Ivinghoe Locks 33 and 34 are set one each side of the next bridge which is double arched. Walk a further ¾ mile amid the flat agricultural landscape and Horton Wharf with the lock and bridge No.121 are reached. Slapton Lock is after bridge No.120.

Bridge No.125 is something of a rarity for there are not many swing bridges along the 147 miles from London to Birmingham. Pass pleasant farmland (left) and the distant Dunstable Downs with Ivinghoe Beacon (right).

From here there are fine views with the distant hills forming a backdrop to the Buckinghamshire farmland (left). The canal bends sharply left and the railway approaches from the right. The moorings of Dunstable and District Boat Club are next on the right just before the canal turns to the right beneath bridge No.126 and the railway line, with the Duke of Wellington pub at Pitstone Wharf.

56

STAGE 5 - BULBOURNE TO THREE LOCKS

Pass beneath the modern concrete road bridge and soon the towpath crosses an old mooring where, across the canal, are rotting remains of landing stages and old piers. On the towpath the remains of the 1920s tramway are still visible. This used to carry sand and gravel from the pits, over to the right, to the canal for shipment.

The canal twists and turns in broad bends through reed beds all the way to Leighton Buzzard. The River Ouzel flows close at bridge No.116 where a small chapel lends its name to lock 29, Church Lock. Cross the bridge and join the towpath on the right of the canal. In 1/4 mile comes Grove Lock. A wide bend right, then left and with the River Ouzel hugging the towpath the noises and industrial development show that we are fast approaching Leighton Buzzard.

Slapton
S.PH.PO.

STAGE 5: 3
Bulbourne to Three Locks

THE GRAND UNION CANAL WALK

STAGE 5: 4
Bulbourne to Three Locks

The canal narrows and passes, on the bend, an old, disused swing bridge (left). At bridge No.111 is the picturesque Globe Inn. Flowing between high trees on both banks, twisting right and left, the canal continues on its way. Before the next bridge a church and Manor Farm become visible. Soon the canal straightens. Gorse bushes grow along the left bank with open meadows and woodland beyond the towpath. The railway comes close again after bridge No.109 and the land sweeps upwards (left) beyond the towpath. After bridge No.108 a high hedge shields the towpath from the farmland beyond and bridge No.107 marks the end of this stage as the Three Locks at Soulbury are reached.

Large willow trees sweep the water and beyond the disused railway bridge the occupants of the houses enjoy long gardens that border the canal. After the white footbridge an attractive church spire is visible among the trees (right). A cricket ground (left) comes next and industry begins to encroach. The towpath crosses a humpback bridge over the entrance to a canal dock of yesteryear. Bending to the right, the canal passes beneath bridge No.114 at Leighton Road and into the Leighton Linslade Moorings. Tesco's and the new Waterfront Bar are close by. Eventually the canal continues past the Wyvern Shipping Company on the opposite bank. With hedges (right) and trees (left) you come to Leighton Lock.

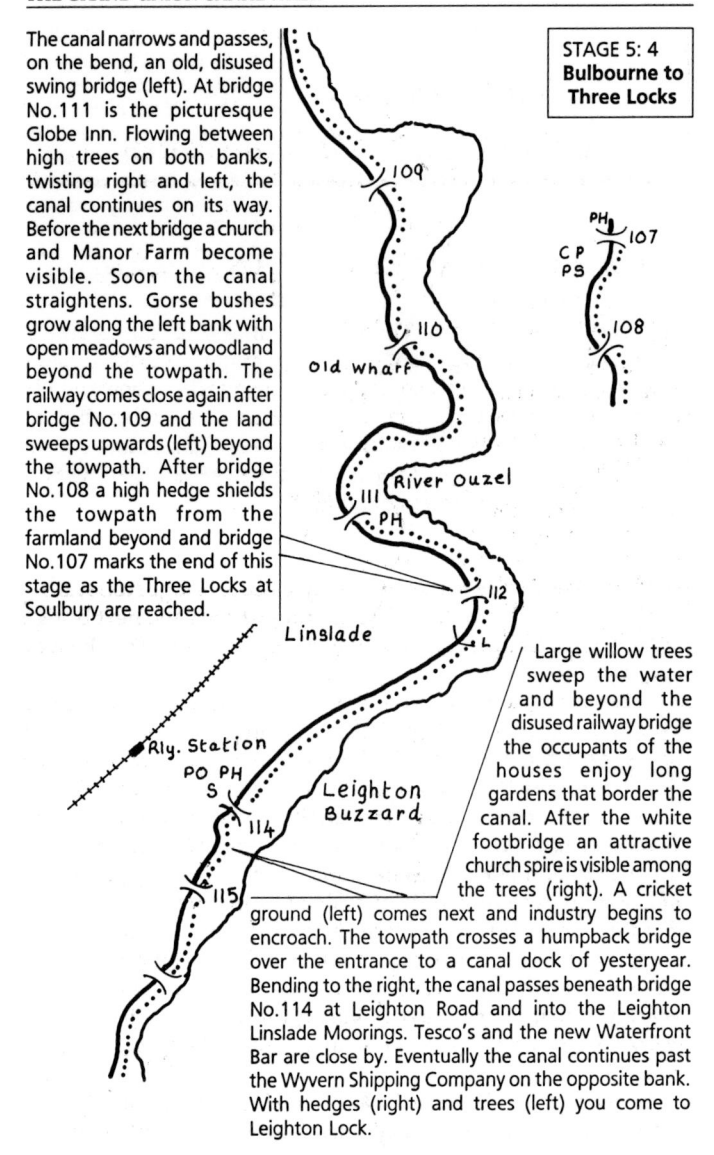

58

STAGE 6:
Soulbury Three Locks to Gifford Park, Milton Keynes

PLACES AND POINTS OF INTEREST ALONG THE WAY

Soulbury Three Locks
Right beside the locks is the Three Locks pub and close by is the old pumphouse now restored and selling all manner of things. In days when the canal was used commercially the working boat people said that these locks were haunted. The reasons seem rather obscure but it was said that a woman and her child haunted the place and on certain nights the squeak of ghostly pram wheels could be heard - I'll leave the rest to your imagination.

Bletchley and Fenny Stratford
At the southern extremities of Bletchley, close to bridge No.99, is the official boundary of Milton Keynes and just after the next bridge No.98 the canal is carried across a tributary of the River Tove by way of an aqueduct.

Like so many other towns today Bletchley and Fenny Stratford are almost joined together as one place although many years ago they formed two very individual communities. One peculiar ritual from the past is the traditional cannon firing in the churchyard known as 'Fenny Poppers'. The tradition is carried out on 11th November each year to celebrate the founding of the church by Dr Browne Willis in 1730. There are numerous shops, eating places and pubs within close proximity of bridge No.96 just north of which, after the railway bridge, is Fenny Stratford Lock. This lock is quite unusual as it has a drop of barely 12 inches, hardly worth the effort you may think, but in fact vital as when it was first built the canal section just to the north was continually losing water. The problem was solved by installing this lock thus allowing the canal level to be lowered.

Nowadays the old swing bridge is rarely swung but it still looks a rather grand piece of engineering left over from another age.

Woughton on the Green

Woughton is another of the villages which have been surrounded by new town development. It has not, however, lost its old world charm. It is spread around a large village green and still has the village pub, The Old Swan. The Milton Keynes Marina is close by, shortly after bridge No.90, and the Open University at Walton Hall is just to the east.

Milton Keynes

Although not everyone's idea of the ideal place to live Milton Keynes certainly has much going for it. The planners created over the last quarter of a century a city of houses, shops, offices, factories, parkland and lakes all landscaped and linked by road and footpath and covering in total about 22,000 acres. They have done their best to preserve the villages that already existed before this vast development scheme began, although these villages are now encompassed by architecture which is in the main ultra modern. The city, with a population of over 100,000, boasts a shopping centre to match the best in Europe and its leisure facilities, both indoor and outdoor, are the envy of many a European. Its parkland near Willen Lake contains such contrasts as the first Buddhist Peace Pagoda in the western hemisphere and a village church dedicated to St Mary Magdalene which is said to be the only Wren church outside London. Through all of this flows the Grand Union Canal.

Great Linford Brick Kilns

The two late 19th century kilns at The Dell were built by George Osborn Price who was a local merchant selling a variety of goods ranging from seed to lime and coal. The bricks produced at Linford were used in the construction of numerous local developments until a few years before the outbreak of the First World War and were shipped as canal cargoes from the wharf nearby to New Bradwell, Wolverton, Castlethorpe and Cosgrove.

STAGE 6 - SOULBURY THREE LOCKS TO GIFFORD PARK, MILTON KEYNES

Working barge and leisure craft at Stoke Hammond

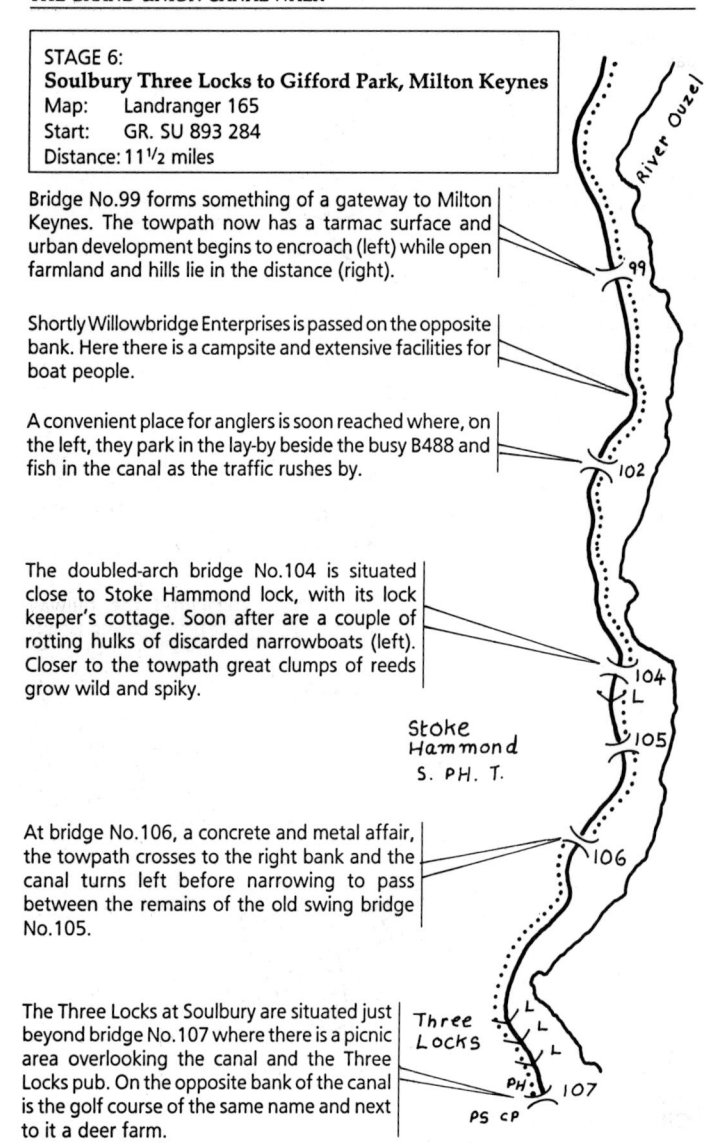

THE GRAND UNION CANAL WALK

STAGE 6:
Soulbury Three Locks to Gifford Park, Milton Keynes
Map: Landranger 165
Start: GR. SU 893 284
Distance: 11½ miles

Bridge No.99 forms something of a gateway to Milton Keynes. The towpath now has a tarmac surface and urban development begins to encroach (left) while open farmland and hills lie in the distance (right).

Shortly Willowbridge Enterprises is passed on the opposite bank. Here there is a campsite and extensive facilities for boat people.

A convenient place for anglers is soon reached where, on the left, they park in the lay-by beside the busy B488 and fish in the canal as the traffic rushes by.

The doubled-arch bridge No.104 is situated close to Stoke Hammond lock, with its lock keeper's cottage. Soon after are a couple of rotting hulks of discarded narrowboats (left). Closer to the towpath great clumps of reeds grow wild and spiky.

At bridge No.106, a concrete and metal affair, the towpath crosses to the right bank and the canal turns left before narrowing to pass between the remains of the old swing bridge No.105.

The Three Locks at Soulbury are situated just beyond bridge No.107 where there is a picnic area overlooking the canal and the Three Locks pub. On the opposite bank of the canal is the golf course of the same name and next to it a deer farm.

62

STAGE 6 - SOULBURY THREE LOCKS TO GIFFORD PARK, MILTON KEYNES

At Simpson village you pass the Plough Inn (right). Soon a marker states 'Braunston 37 miles', then comes an old brick bridge No.91 with the modern plate 'Milton Keynes New Town' on it.

Continue under the A5(T) and bridge No.92, a more traditional brick structure which makes a pleasant change after the white concrete of the new town.

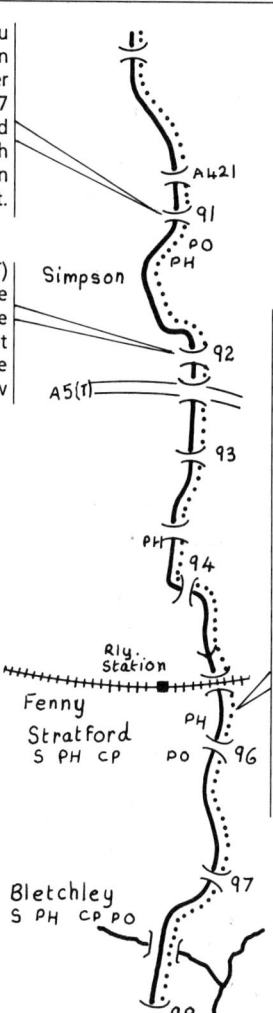

The canal now passes along an embankment with a housing estate below (left). 'Braunston 39 miles' is marked just before bridge No.97. After passing a small lifting bridge, with a modern marina (right), you reach bridge No.96 with the Bridge Inn (left) at Fenny Stratford. Beyond the railway bridge, the Red Lion is across the canal to the left of the locks. Industrial estates continue after bridge No.94 where the canal turns right with the main road now on its right.

STAGE 6: 2
Soulbury Three Locks to Gifford Park, Milton Keynes

63

THE GRAND UNION CANAL WALK

> **STAGE 6: 3**
> **Soulbury Three Locks to Gifford Park, Milton Keynes**

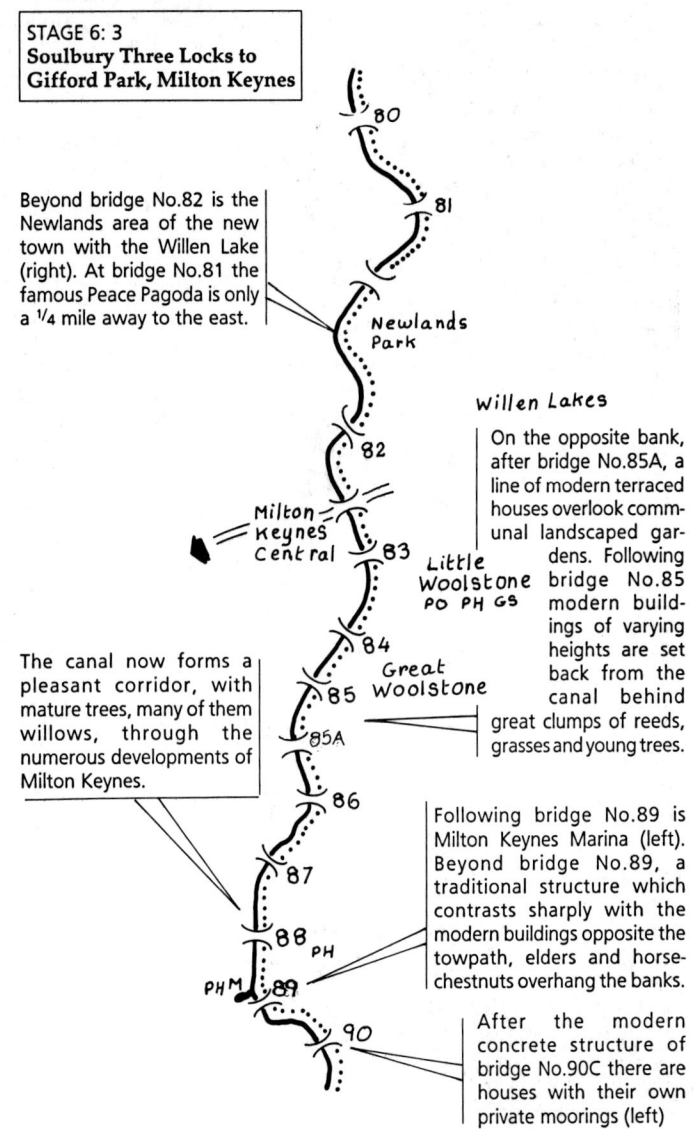

Beyond bridge No.82 is the Newlands area of the new town with the Willen Lake (right). At bridge No.81 the famous Peace Pagoda is only a ¼ mile away to the east.

Newlands Park

Willen Lakes

On the opposite bank, after bridge No.85A, a line of modern terraced houses overlook communal landscaped gardens. Following bridge No.85 modern buildings of varying heights are set back from the canal behind great clumps of reeds, grasses and young trees.

Milton Keynes Central

Little Woolstone PO PH GS

Great Woolstone

The canal now forms a pleasant corridor, with mature trees, many of them willows, through the numerous developments of Milton Keynes.

Following bridge No.89 is Milton Keynes Marina (left). Beyond bridge No.89, a traditional structure which contrasts sharply with the modern buildings opposite the towpath, elders and horse-chestnuts overhang the banks.

After the modern concrete structure of bridge No.90C there are houses with their own private moorings (left)

64

STAGE 6 - SOULBURY THREE LOCKS TO GIFFORD PARK, MILTON KEYNES

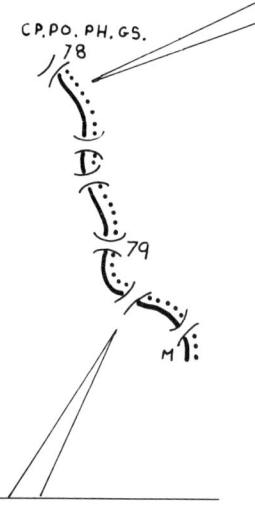

The old bridge No.78, at Gifford Park, only stands as a result of a protest by the residents of the new town; it was reprieved from demolition as part of the Milton Keynes masterplan, and now carries modern decking in place of the old road surface. Immediately after this bridge the Gifford Park pub, situated beside the towpath, brings this section of the journey to an end.

The canal turns left, then left again, before passing bridges Nos.80 and 79A with Pennyland Marina and the Lionheart Cruising Club (left). Next to the towpath is parkland, willow trees and well-groomed hawthorn hedges. Bridge No.79 is a mixture of old brick and new concrete. Further on, on the opposite side of the canal, are the old brick kilns.

STAGE 6: 3 continued
Soulbury Three Locks to Gifford Park, Milton Keynes

STAGE 7:
Gifford Park, Milton Keynes to Stoke Bruerne

PLACES AND POINTS OF INTEREST ALONG THE WAY

Gifford Park and Linford Village

Gifford Park is a good example of new town urban development, with modern shops and a public house set beside the old canal. Previously there was little else apart from fields; now the place is a modern suburbia but the pleasant old remains of history are just to the east, along the towpath at Linford.

Beyond the bridge No.77 the canal stretches out straight for almost ½ mile and on its southern bank is Linford Manor Park. Amongst the trees the 13th-century church of St Andrew stands on slightly raised ground overseeing the almshouses lower down the hill. These were the homes for six unmarried poor people of the parish during the 17th century and were built by Sir William Pritchard, Lord Mayor of London, who decided that Great Linford was to be his main country seat. They are somewhat unusual dwellings in that they consist of a row of single-storey homes with a two-storey centre; this at one time served as the local school.

The Manor House, set at 90 degrees to the almshouses and to the church, looks out over well manicured parklands which were extensively landscaped during the 18th century at the same time that the old house itself was carefully extended.

It is interesting to note that as recently as 1982 a meadow of wild flowers was created outside the churchyard and as a result cowslips, woolley thistles, ox-eye daisies and knapweed flourish here and they in turn help to attract a wide range of insect, butterfly and birdlife to this peaceful parkland amidst the new town.

Close to the edge of the park is the old village of Great Linford, a mixture of brick and stone buildings with slate and thatched roofs and the large white building of The Nags Head, with its high thatched roof.

Newport Pagnell

Only a couple of miles to the north-east of Linford is Newport Pagnell, formerly a small, quiet Midlands town but today almost part of Milton Keynes. During the English Civil War the Parliamentarians garrisoned the town and trained their recruits here and it is believed that John Bunyan, the most famous son of Elstow in Bedfordshire, was one of those who volunteered at the tender age of 16 years. John Bunyan was an extremely strong Nonconformist and was later to become famous as the author of *A Pilgrim's Progress*. Cromwell's second son, who was a garrison captain at Newport Pagnell, died not in battle but of smallpox.

New Bradwell

New Bradwell was originally developed during the mid 1800s as a village to house the families of those employed at the London and North Western Railway workshops at nearby Wolverton. Little remains today of the 180 terraced, two-storey red brick houses as the majority were demolished to make way for the new town 20 years ago. The village church survived but apart from having a Norman chancel arch taken from the ruined church at Stantonbury built into its west wall, it has little else of interest.

Bradwell, Ancient and Modern

Progressing along Grafton Street Aqueduct the walker can feel that beneath the feet lies a rare combination of the old and the new; for this impressive modern aqueduct is the first to have been built on the canal system for a good 50 years and proved to be one of the most complicated pieces of civil engineering in the development of Milton Keynes.

Before you get half way across the aqueduct turn round and admire the view. In the distance, amongst the trees, you can make out the shape of Bradwell Mill. Unlike the bordering counties of East Anglia, Buckinghamshire is not well endowed with windmills so this one is a rarity. As recently as 1803 Samuel Halman purchased an acre of land on which to build a Smock Mill. The mill never flourished as a financial venture and it had various owners until 1876 when the railway company bought the adjacent land just to the north of it. This brought to an end the commercial milling at Bradwell. The Milton Keynes Development Corporation bought the mill in 1969 since when it has undergone extensive restoration.

Bradwell Abbey

In 1154 the Baron of Wolverton, Meinfelin, gave land to the Benedictine monks at Luffield Abbey so that they might found a priory at Bradwell. Unfortunately the coming of the Black Death contributed to limiting development in the locality and by 1349 not much was left of the venture. However the priory struggled on, earning its keep by various means, for a further 200 years or so until 1524 when the lands and the priory were donated to Cardinal Wolsey toward his new college at Oxford. Later the site passed to Sheen Priory but soon Sheen itself suffered at the hands of Henry VIII during his Dissolution of the Monasteries. There is an extra twist to the tale, for only in recent years has evidence of the former importance of Bradwell Abbey all those years ago come to light with discovery of the original seal of the priory at Wolverton. It is now thought that Sir John Longville, who was patron of the priory, may well have taken the seal for safe-keeping during those turbulent times to his home at Wolverton.

Fuel for the stove near bridge No. 75

Wolverton

As New Bradwell was created as a dormitory village for the railway workers, so Wolverton was developed as a working railway town. Its first railway station was opened in 1838 along with the carriage and locomotive workshops. A second station followed a couple of years later as business flourished and for about a hundred years it continued as a centre for railway engineering. Although not as busy today as in its heyday, a new industrial development is re-using former railway land.

Access to the railway station and to the town is from the canal towpath at bridge No.71, beneath which is an information board on which details of Wolverton are displayed.

Stony Stratford

Today's town, just a few miles west of Wolverton, is itself part of the new town of Milton Keynes but its development goes back to the days of coach travel when it became an important staging post. Its broad High Street, filled with red brick Georgian houses, is in fact part of the old Roman road to Holyhead, namely Watling Street. Two old inns on the High Street, The Cock and The Bull, have left their mark on the English language, for at these inns stories were told that were just too outrageous to be believed; no doubt the tales were spread by the coachmen and so they became known as 'Cock and Bull' stories.

The Iron Trunk Aqueduct

The canal crosses the River Great Ouse at the lowest point between Braunston and Tring, consequently the canal company's engineer decided to cross the deep Ouse valley by building up embankments and placing aqueducts across the river. An alternative method would have been to construct a series of locks with bridges or some kind of ferry to take the horses which pulled the narrowboats; clearly this method would have been expensive and very time-consuming, therefore the former method was chosen. To enable the canal to continue working during the construction period a flight of temporary locks built from wood were sited to the south of the river. The remains of these locks are still visible today and the lock at Cosgrove, a little further up the towpath, was part of the original flight.

THE GRAND UNION CANAL WALK

Walkers heading south beside the Iron Trunk Aqueduct with the River Great Ouse far below

When the building was started the project was not considered unusually difficult but it soon became apparent that it was not going to be as straightforward as originally thought. Well before 1805 there had been a series of problems but on 18th February disaster struck when the whole thing collapsed into the valley below. The temporary lock system was hastily brought back into use to prevent disruption to the canal's trade; meanwhile it was decided that the replacement aqueduct should be made of cast iron. The 'Iron Trunk', as it was called, was designed by a local engineer, Benjamin Bevan, and was manufactured in the Midlands iron works of the Reynolds Company. Apart from maintenance work carried out in 1921 and 1986, there has been no interruption of canal traffic since its completion in 1811.

Cosgrove

The rivers Tove and the better known Ouse form boundaries for the old village of Cosgrove which was originally settled during Roman times. Until the early 1800s it was something of a rural backwater but then Cosgrove found itself at the junction of the main canal and the branch to Buckingham, thus its importance was assured whilst the canal was busy. Today little remains of the Stratford and Buckingham branch canal except for about 150 yards of water over to the left as you reach Cosgrove Marina. Originally when the branch was opened in 1801 it stretched for over 10 miles and had two locks. The cargoes carried on it were mainly hay and straw for London where, at the time, with so much horse-drawn traffic on its streets, the capital's appetite for horse fodder seemed endless. The canal trade was also helped by the substantial development of a small boatyard at Old Stratford. It was founded in 1840 and the boat building reputation of the Edward Hays Yards became well known internationally. His launches, steam boats, tugs and harbour vessels found their way all over the globe, many being manufactured in sections and assembled on reaching their destination. Some of them came along the canal under their own steam but if size and draught made this impossible they would be transported in sections as canal cargo. The boatyards closed between the two World Wards at a time when the canal to Buckingham was already in a run down state and it was finally abandoned in 1961.

The building of the North Buckinghamshire and South

THE GRAND UNION CANAL WALK

The Grand Union at Cosgrove

Northamptonshire stretch of the M1 motorway finally worked out the large gravel and sand deposits nearby. Since then the vast craters have been turned into the huge leisure park of Cosgrove Lodge which boasts seven lakes, a funfair, café, bar, swimming facilities and a shop within its 110 acres. It can be seen from the towpath over to the right as Cosgrove Marina is approached from the south.

Closer to the village and in a field behind the old National school is St Vincent's Well which is protected by an Act of Parliament. The water from the well is rich in iron and said to have certain healing properties, especially for eye troubles. The village pub is the Barley Mow and is well worth a visit.

Cosgrove Priory is the village's 'grand' house and was the home of the Atkinsons who were great village benefactors. Close by the house stood a water mill which was still in use until the 1920s but has since been demolished. It was said that many years ago a daughter of the house fell in love with a local shepherd and as her family disapproved of him they decided to have him deported on a false charge of sheep stealing. On learning of his fate their daughter threw herself into the mill race and her ghost is said to haunt the area at full moon.

THE GRAND UNION CANAL WALK

Castlethorpe

Leaving behind the rather unusual Gothic form of Solomon's bridge (the reason for its elaborate 1800s design seems to be something of a mystery), the village of Castlethorpe can be seen about a mile away to the north-east. Between the canal and the village is the River Tove and the railway line. On the northern side of the village is the grey stone, slate roofed church of St Simon and St Jude, dating back to Norman times. Its tower collapsed during the 1700s and was replaced with its present tower which is Georgian in style. Just to the west of the church are the remains of a medieval motte and bailey castle. The village itself consists of the village pub, The Carrington Arms, the general store and a collection of stone and colour washed cottages closely lining its streets.

Hanslope

Beyond Castlethorpe lies Hanslope with its church steeple clearly visible as Thrupp is approached. St James's church boasts the finest steeple in the county; it is certainly a landmark for many miles around. The village sits on a low ridge amidst the arable land of north Buckinghamshire and consists of two parallel main streets. Many of its dwellings are 17th and 18th century stone buildings, some of which are thatched.

Yardley Gobion

From Yardley Wharf the village is but a few minutes' walk from the towpath; just cross the bridge and follow the lane to the south where Yardley Gobion is tucked away close to the southern tip of Northamptonshire. Within the parish is the Queen's Oak where it is said King Edward IV met Elizabeth Woodville whom he later married and they became parents to the ill fated 'Princes in the Tower.'

During the 14th and 15th centuries it had a thriving pottery manufacturing business, evidence of which was found during the village's expansion, but today it is a 'dormitory' village. One of its pubs has survived from the old days and has the unusual name of The Coffee Pot.

Potterspury

About the same size as Yardley Gobion and situated just beyond it is Potterspury. The name of the village was changed during the 12th century as it better reflected its connection with the manufacture of pottery. As with its neighbour, Yardley Gobion, evidence of a substantial industry for its period in history has come to light over the years. Before it achieved its reputation for pottery it was known as Estpirie or Pyrie, which was derived from Pyrige. This indicated that it was a pear producing area but presumably there was more money to be made from pottery.

Nearby, the Dukes of Grafton lived at Wakefield Lodge from about 1748 until 1918. The second duke engaged William Kent to build his house on the site of the former hunting lodge in Whittlebury Forest, the landscaping being completed by Capability Brown.

There used to be six pubs in the village but today only two remain; The Cock and The Talbot are still here to quench the villagers' thirst.

As the railway workshops at Wolverton expanded many of the menfolk found employment there while the women of Potterspury mainly worked as lacemakers. During the mid 1800s over 130 females from the village were employed in this trade, some of them still only children.

Now converted to private dwellings, the village mill continued to grind corn until 50 years ago. Originally its power source was a small but useful stream that still flows through the village.

Grafton Regis

Squeezed in between the A5 (Watling Street) and a bend in the canal is the rather grand-sounding Grafton Regis. Today's village is but a sprinkle of dwellings, a few farms, the rectory and The White Hart pub. The lands of the manor house have been traced back to early 12th century. During his reign Henry VIII and Ann Boleyn visited the manor, which today is a hospital, and the word 'Regis' was added to the village's name of Grafton. Later again, the title of Dukedom of Grafton was conferred on his illegitimate son, Henry Fitzroy, by Charles II. In the 12th-century church the font is Norman and the monuments to the Fitzroy family are numerous.

Stoke Bruerne

The bottom lock, of Stoke Bruerne's flight of seven, is quite picturesque and overlooked by ivy-clad cottages where years ago

The bridge at Yardley Wharf.
(Caution elderly ducks crossing)

its wharfs were busy with loading and unloading. Just a little further up the flight, close to the sixth lock, the remains of the old brickworks are still recognisable.

Much of the property at Stoke Bruerne was owned by the Duke of Grafton. Ninety years ago the population was not much more than it is today, in spite of the canal trade, the brickworks and the local railway. Today the main business is the tourist trade, for it caters well for those who come to enjoy its pleasant blend of attractive quaintness and industrial history. Britain's first Canal Museum is housed in the former mill building situated on the quayside. It was opened in 1963 and by the mid 1980s a million visitors had passed through it. Still very popular, it contains a vast array of colourful memorabilia of canal life including photographs, clothing, engines, china and painted ware, all of which serve to illustrate what life was like on the canal in the days gone by. The well extended village pub, aptly named Boat Inn, stretches from the quay into the village centre, while on the opposite quay, a few doors down from the museum, is the Bruerne's Lock restaurant. A tearoom in a former church is just beyond the museum and close to the car park.

Almost immediately the canal bears right and after the railway bridge No.71A the Milton Keynes branch of the Inland Waterways Association have painted a mural along the wall of the opposite bank which depicts transport. It also gives various distances: Brentford 74 miles south, Cosgrove 2 miles north, Stoke Bruerne 8 miles north and Birmingham now a mere 72 miles away.

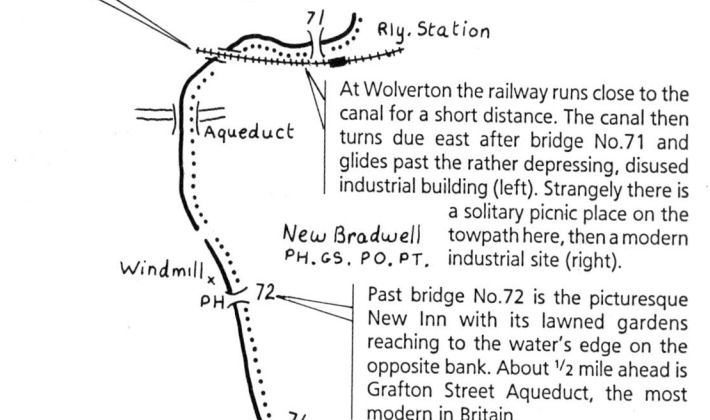

At Wolverton the railway runs close to the canal for a short distance. The canal then turns due east after bridge No.71 and glides past the rather depressing, disused industrial building (left). Strangely there is a solitary picnic place on the towpath here, then a modern industrial site (right).

Past bridge No.72 is the picturesque New Inn with its lawned gardens reaching to the water's edge on the opposite bank. About ½ mile ahead is Grafton Street Aqueduct, the most modern in Britain.

Pass an entrance to the Wildfowl Trust (right) then under bridge No.74 where the towpath passes through the Bradwell area of Milton Keynes. Here some of the new homes, across the canal, have their own jetty with a private narrowboat moored alongside.

Shortly the lakes of the Wildfowl Trust become visible over to the right. Pass a bridleway, followed by the distance indicator reading 31 miles to Braunston (right) before bridge No.75

STAGE 7:
Gifford Park, Milton Keynes to Stoke Bruerne
Map: Landranger 152
Start: GR. SP 861 424
Distance: 12½ miles

At bridge No.77 leave the towpath and cross the bridge over to the left should you wish to visit Great Linford, after which continue along the towpath, passing the Black Horse Hotel (right) before going beneath the modern road bridge No.76, which carries the Newport Pagnell to Wolverton road.

Bridge No.78 can clearly be seen from the road at Gifford Park Shopping Centre. Join the towpath behind the Gifford Park pub and walk eastwards with the canal (left) and bridge No.78 behind.

THE GRAND UNION CANAL WALK

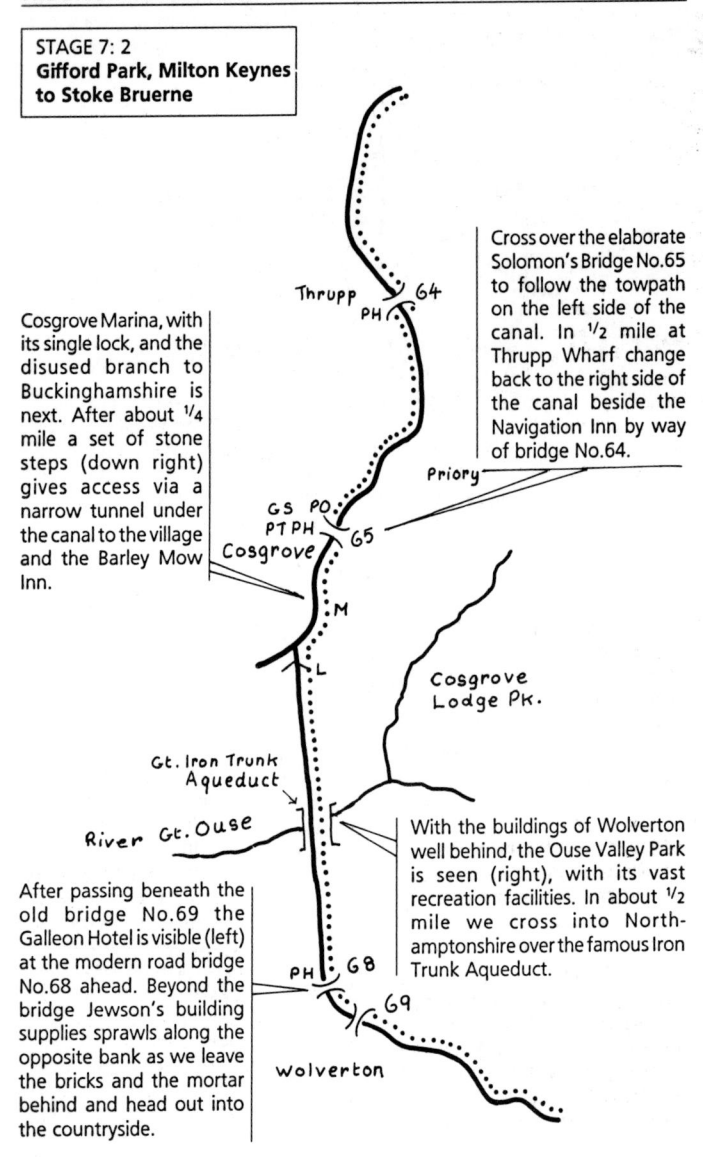

> **STAGE 7: 2**
> **Gifford Park, Milton Keynes to Stoke Bruerne**

Cosgrove Marina, with its single lock, and the disused branch to Buckinghamshire is next. After about ¼ mile a set of stone steps (down right) gives access via a narrow tunnel under the canal to the village and the Barley Mow Inn.

Cross over the elaborate Solomon's Bridge No.65 to follow the towpath on the left side of the canal. In ½ mile at Thrupp Wharf change back to the right side of the canal beside the Navigation Inn by way of bridge No.64.

With the buildings of Wolverton well behind, the Ouse Valley Park is seen (right), with its vast recreation facilities. In about ½ mile we cross into Northamptonshire over the famous Iron Trunk Aqueduct.

After passing beneath the old bridge No.69 the Galleon Hotel is visible (left) at the modern road bridge No.68 ahead. Beyond the bridge Jewson's building supplies sprawls along the opposite bank as we leave the bricks and the mortar behind and head out into the countryside.

78

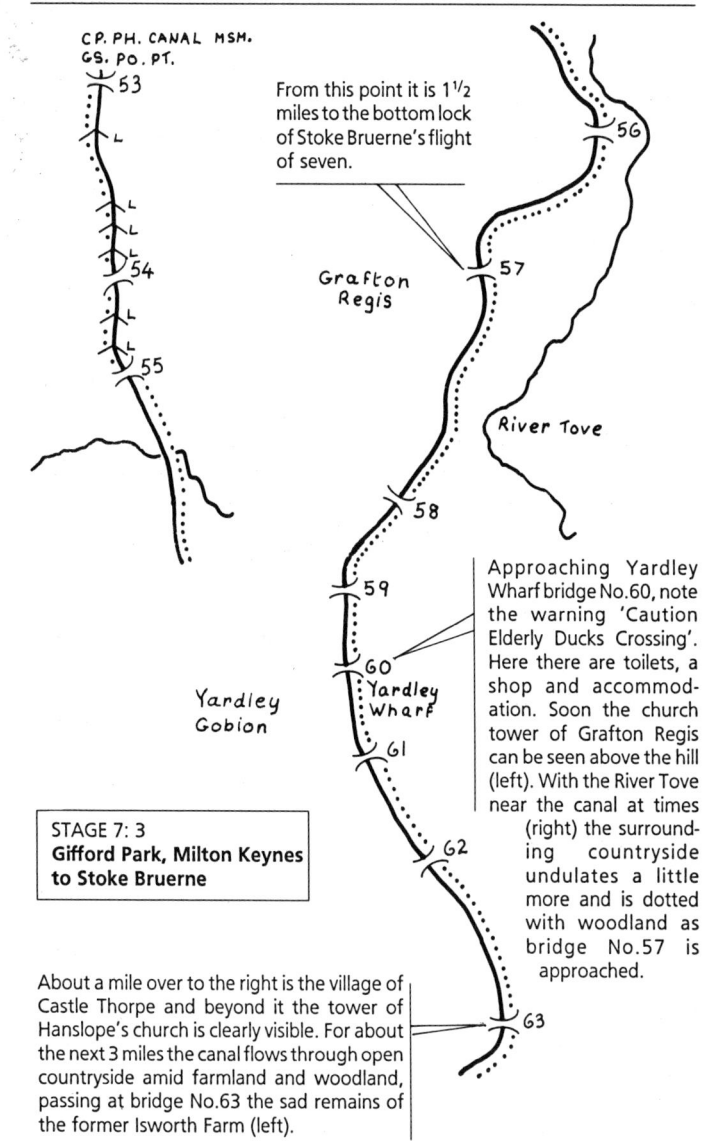

STAGE 7 - GIFFORD PARK, MILTON KEYNES TO STOKE BRUERNE

CP. PH. CANAL MSM.
GS. PO. PT.

From this point it is 1½ miles to the bottom lock of Stoke Bruerne's flight of seven.

Grafton Regis

River Tove

Yardley Gobion

STAGE 7: 3
Gifford Park, Milton Keynes to Stoke Bruerne

Approaching Yardley Wharf bridge No.60, note the warning 'Caution Elderly Ducks Crossing'. Here there are toilets, a shop and accommodation. Soon the church tower of Grafton Regis can be seen above the hill (left). With the River Tove near the canal at times (right) the surrounding countryside undulates a little more and is dotted with woodland as bridge No.57 is approached.

About a mile over to the right is the village of Castle Thorpe and beyond it the tower of Hanslope's church is clearly visible. For about the next 3 miles the canal flows through open countryside amid farmland and woodland, passing at bridge No.63 the sad remains of the former Isworth Farm (left).

79

STAGE 8:
Stoke Bruerne to Weedon

PLACES AND POINTS OF INTEREST ALONG THE WAY

Blisworth and Blisworth Tunnel

Ironstone workings were once very common in the area and there were many limekilns hereabouts, but the greatest impact made upon the village of Blisworth and the surrounding hamlets was certainly the coming of the canal age.

Its importance as a canalside village really became apparent when it was realised that the village was right alongside the proposed northern end of a tunnel that had to be constructed if the canal was to progress at all in this part of the Midlands. Jubilation indeed when the chief engineer of the time, William Jessop, made his quite incorrect and sweeping statement that he had never come across ground more suitable for tunnelling than that at Blisworth.

He began work in 1793 and after many frustrations and two years' time he considered abandoning his original plan and building a series of locks to carry the canal across the hill instead. His construction supervisor responsible for the tunnel was one James Barnes, an engineer noted for his ability to persevere. This he did but the canal had been open and functioning for ten years when the tunnel, all 3,056 yards of it, was at last open for traffic. During this time a tramway had been built to connect Blisworth with Stoke Bruerne, thus a complete route, in spite of the difficulties at Blisworth tunnel, had been completed between London and the industrial heartland of the Midlands at Birmingham.

Many of Blisworth's menfolk - the young, the fit and the healthy - became 'leggers'. These were a new generation of men who, as canal tunnels were developed throughout the country, found an agreeable but tough way of earning their living by lying on their backs on the deck or hatch cover of the narrowboats and then walking on the roof or sides of the tunnels thereby propelling the craft along. With the introduction of the tug boats in the early 1870s the leggers' usefulness became obsolete and up to 25 narrowboats strung together in a long convoy could be towed by one of the new generation of tugs, which were finally phased out here in 1936.

The village of Blisworth is a pleasant enough place. It has a lot of modern residential development but architecturally the great warehouse built of brick in 1879 by the then Grand Junction Canal Company is quite outstanding.

Many of the older thatched village houses date from the 16th century and the combination of local ironstone with Northamptonshire sandstone in alternative courses gives some dwelling a pleasant combination of light and dark lines to their exterior walls.

Bugbrooke

This rather unfortunately named village, just to the east of the canal, had the name of 'Buchebroc' at the time of Domesday and during more recent times, about a hundred years ago in fact, it boasted the first soap factory in England. Then it must have been quite a prosperous place, having its own brickyard, more than one local mill and a number of bakeries and other trades necessary to support the lives of the thriving village community. Today the large Heygate Mill still operates and dominates the skyline on the banks of the River Nene, otherwise the main business of the area is farming.

The village has developed over the last 30 years or so but the old part of the village retains its connections with days gone by. This is particularly so with the 14th-century church that dominates this part of the village and inside of which is a very fine 15th-century wooden screen, one of the very few remaining in this part of England.

Nether Heyford

"Take away the Lady Jane from me." These words were from the lament of Heyford's most infamous character, Judge Francis Morgan of the King's Bench. It was he who pronounced the death sentence on Lady Jane Grey and then, broken with remorse, committed suicide in 1558. A monument showing him kneeling at an altar with his wife and family appears on the south wall of the village church.

A more popular local figure was William Bliss who, in 1674, endowed the local school with £400. The main feature of today's village, which is but a short distance from bridge No.32, is the enormous tree-lined green; the largest in the area it covers some 5 acres.

THE GRAND UNION CANAL WALK

This part of the towpath is quite narrow and overhung with trees. Just before Blisworth Mill at bridge No.51 there is a mooring. After the bridge the towpath improves and back gardens are close by (right).

After bridge No.50, Candle Bridge, the countryside opens out into a gently rolling scene and the canal passes under a road bridge, then a railway bridge, followed by a further road bridge. At bridge No.48 cross to the left of the canal.

Leave the road, go down the bridleway opposite and turn immediately right onto the concrete surface to join the towpath outside the tunnel's northern entrance. From here you are approximately 2 miles from Stoke Bruerne.

STAGE 8:
Stoke Bruerne to Weedon
Map: Landranger 152
Start: GR. SP 745 499
Distance: 12¼ miles

At the road junction coming from the right, follow the sign towards Blisworth. On reaching a bend in the road look for the solid Georgian-type house with the unusual name of Blisworth Stone Works (right).

At the road junction coming from the left, continue walking ahead along the road. From here the circular, brick-built air shafts, which ventilate the tunnel below, are clearly visible in the direction of Blisworth. Pass Buttermilk Hall Farm (left) where there is a Camping and Caravan Club site.

Leave Stoke Bruerne walking along the towpath with the Canal Museum (right). Before the entrance to the Blisworth Tunnel, through which there is no towpath, you must take the footpath to the right and climb up over the tunnel. As you do so you pass between the brick piers that carried the old railway line. At the top of the hill continue along the path amid the trees until reaching the road.

STAGE 8 - STOKE BRUERNE TO WEEDON

STAGE 8: 2
Stoke Bruerne to Weedon

Aqueduct

For the next few miles the railway is never far away on the left of the canal. Sometimes the trains are only heard and not seen as they speed noisily by in both directions across embankments and under bridges.

Gayton

Near bridge No.46 the towpath narrows and the railway is almost within touching distance. Just before the canal runs between shallow embankments, swathed in greenery, the tower of the church at Gayton is visible (left).

At bridge No.47 cross back to the right of the canal. This bridge is now used for road traffic but it was also used by the horses, who towed the narrowboats, in order to gain access to the opposite towpath by way of the gradual climbing curve.

Rothersthorpe

Gayton Junction

PT.
PH

You are now at Gayton Junction with 16½ miles to go to Braunston. To the right is the Northampton Arm of the canal, the Grand Junction Boat Company, a small shop, a toilet and extensive moorings.

83

THE GRAND UNION CANAL WALK

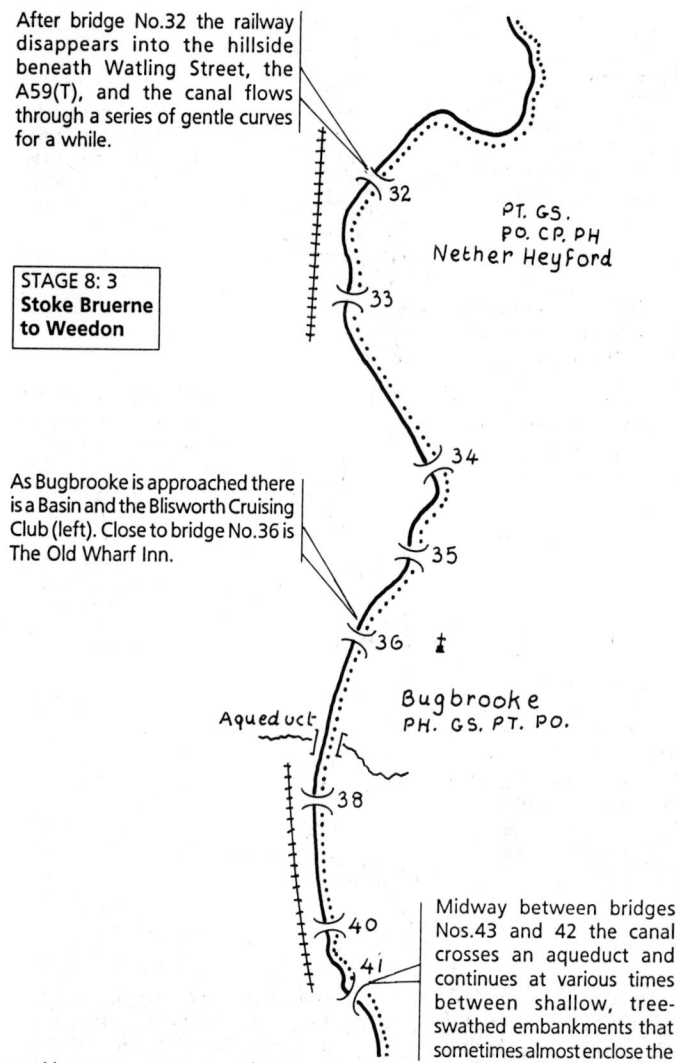

After bridge No.32 the railway disappears into the hillside beneath Watling Street, the A59(T), and the canal flows through a series of gentle curves for a while.

**STAGE 8: 3
Stoke Bruerne
to Weedon**

PT. GS.
PO. CP. PH
Nether Heyford

As Bugbrooke is approached there is a Basin and the Blisworth Cruising Club (left). Close to bridge No.36 is The Old Wharf Inn.

Aqueduct

Bugbrooke
PH. GS. PT. PO.

Midway between bridges Nos.43 and 42 the canal crosses an aqueduct and continues at various times between shallow, tree-swathed embankments that sometimes almost enclose the canal in greenery. In autumn the leaves produce a spectacular display of colour for mile after mile. At other times the canal flows between gently rolling hills and arable farmland.

STAGE 8 - STOKE BRUERNE TO WEEDON

The towpath narrows and weeds grow in abundance. After bridge No.25 the Nene Way runs, for a short distance, along the towpath. Soon the canal broadens and Weedon Wharf clings to the left bank. The Nene Way disappears down to the right and St Peter's church is passed (left). From Weedon Boatyard and Marina it is 9 miles to Braunston. Immediately before bridge No.24, which carries the noisy A45, is the Village Antique market (right).

The canal curves to the left and then to the right beneath bridge No.27 at Flore Lane Wharf. Here the old industrial buildings have been converted into private dwellings. Past Stowe Marina (left) you approach bridge No.26, which carries the A5, Watling Street.

To the left of bridge No.28, up gently sloping fields, is a collection of handsome Northamptonshire brick-built farm buildings. Beyond the bridge a campsite, in a meadow, reaches down to the water's edge.

STAGE 8: 4
Stoke Bruerne to Weedon

Bridge 27 at Flore Lane Wharf

STAGE 9:
Weedon to Braunston

PLACES AND POINTS OF INTEREST ALONG THE WAY

Weedon Bec

The canal runs right through Weedon, separating the various parts of this quiet rather insignificant village. The name originally derives from the Abbey of Bec Hellouin in Normandy, the holders of the Manor during the 12th century. During the Napoleonic Wars Weedon, with its central location and its proximity to the new mode of water transport, quickly became the home of the Royal Military Depot, in fact a fortification in which George III, with his family, could take refuge, should the situation demand. This new military establishment included stabling for over 200 horses, a riding school, an armoury for 800,000 weapons of war, billeting for two complete regiments of men and all the necessary back-up provisions. The barracks were never visited by him but it remained an army establishment until 1965.

Norton and Long Buckby Wharf

Over to the east of Buckby's bottom lock is the pretty little stone village of Norton built on the same site as the original village before Domesday. During the reign of Elizabeth I Norton Hall was the home of the Knightly family of Fowsley. Unfortunately in 1947 the old hall was blown up as no one could be found to restore it.

Long Buckby stretches for 1^1/$_2$ miles just to the north-east while the tiny hamlet of Long Buckby Wharf is but a scattering of cottages beside the canal as it climbs through the locks to continue its journey almost due west.

Welton

Shortly before the Braunston Tunnel we pass the charming village of Welton which watches over the surrounding countryside from its hilltop vantage point just to the north of the canal. The village church is dedicated to St Martin and contains a tub-shaped font which is said to be Saxon and was dragged here in one piece from

STAGE 9 - WEEDON TO BRAUNSTON

Elegant arches at Braunston

East Anglia.

The main dwelling in the village was Welton Place where the Clarke family lived for over a century. The crown jewellers, the Garrards, later resided here and were visited by members of the royal family on many occasions. When the house was demolished during recent years to make way for modern housing Roman glass, copper and coinage came to light.

Braunston

Like other places on this journey Braunston grew due to its proximity to the canal and was one of the major boat building and repair centres. Those familiar with canal history will know that one of the better known of English narrowboat builders resided here. William Nurser in 1878 opened a narrowboat yard and with the aid of his two sons developed a thriving business that was to continue long after his death.

Braunston Marina is one of the largest in the country. Most of the dock facilities, offices and warehouses that are now part of this complex were left from the days when Braunston was a large trans-shipment base dealing with the commercial traffic on the canal during its heyday. Even today a tremendous number of boats of various size and shape fills the marina, presenting a spectacular and interesting display.

Braunston village is an attractive one especially where 'Dark Lane' runs parallel to the canal near the old inn with its attendant bridge and lock. It is said that here a figure dressed in black walks through the blocked-up doorway and into the inn causing pictures to fall to the ground and glasses in the bar to rattle.

The 2,000 yard long Braunston tunnel was completed and ready for commercial traffic in 1796. Steam tugs were introduced in 1871 and used until 1934.

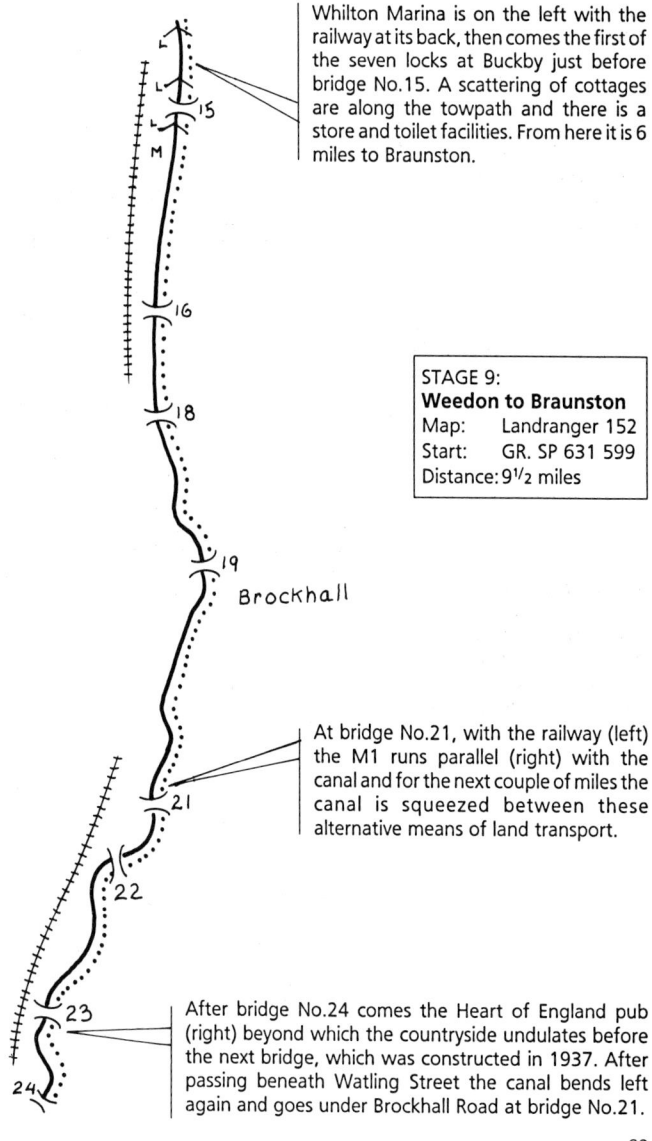

STAGE 9 - WEEDON TO BRAUNSTON

Whilton Marina is on the left with the railway at its back, then comes the first of the seven locks at Buckby just before bridge No.15. A scattering of cottages are along the towpath and there is a store and toilet facilities. From here it is 6 miles to Braunston.

STAGE 9:
Weedon to Braunston
Map: Landranger 152
Start: GR. SP 631 599
Distance: 9½ miles

Brockhall

At bridge No.21, with the railway (left) the M1 runs parallel (right) with the canal and for the next couple of miles the canal is squeezed between these alternative means of land transport.

After bridge No.24 comes the Heart of England pub (right) beyond which the countryside undulates before the next bridge, which was constructed in 1937. After passing beneath Watling Street the canal bends left again and goes under Brockhall Road at bridge No.21.

89

THE GRAND UNION CANAL WALK

As the Braunston Tunnel is approached climb up the concrete track on the left of the entrance. Walk straight ahead passing a small copse of trees and a brick ventilation shaft in the field (left).

STAGE 9: 2
Weedon to Braunston

The towpath surface is quite rough here and there are high hedges (left) and gently rolling farmland (right). The railway is now lost and the motorway forgotten. This is the first time since Weedon that you are free of the noise of traffic except, of course, for the engines of the narrowboats. The canal passes between heavily wooded, high-sided banks. After passing beneath a concrete bridge climb the steps up to the left of the embankment and continue with the canal down below where the old towpath has long since disappeared.

At Norton Junction cross the white footbridge over the Leicester Arm. Pass to the right of the cottage then go over the old bridge No.10 and walk beside the canal as it travels almost due west.

After passing beneath the railway the canal turns left to climb the locks, passing under a further two bridges as it does so. Then comes one of the few additions to the towpath to make walking a little more straightforward: a narrow tunnel beneath the A5(T) at bridge No.11. At the top lock, on the opposite side of the canal, is the New Inn.

90

STAGE 9 - WEEDON TO BRAUNSTON

Shortly before dropping down to the western entrance of the tunnel a third ventilation shaft is passed (right). Climb up the set of steps (left) and a sign reads 'Braunston Top Lock right' (right). Follow the sign along the field edge, with a high hedge (right) to Braunston Top Lock and bridge No.5. Close to bridge No.4 is the Admiral Nelson and the British Waterways Office, formerly the 'Stop House' where the tolls were paid. Continue along the towpath, passing beneath bridge Nos.4, 3, 2 and 1, which are interspersed with locks. After bridge No.91 is the junction, from the north, with the Oxford Canal. Here the water is spanned by a pair of elegant-looking iron bridges.

STAGE 9: 3
Weedon to Braunston

Join the track from the right and continue walking ahead. Cross the A361 then climb up the track to the left of the cottage. After the summit of the hill pass a second brick-built ventilation shaft (right), just the other side of the hedge. A tall, slender church spire points to the sky above the distant Daventry (left).

91

STAGE 10:
Braunston to Radford Semele

PLACES AND POINTS OF INTEREST ALONG THE WAY

Wolfhampcote

The route of the original Oxford Canal is immediately after bridge No.97 although little of it is discernible today. Just to the left of this canal is Wolfhampcote Hall. During the early 1800s there was a 30ft long canal tunnel close to the hall and Wolfhampcote was a thriving village, but not much is left of it now except a few cottages and the restored church.

Napton on the Hill

The population of Napton on the Hill has virtually remained the same since the Middle Ages when it was one of three large towns in the county. During the 14th century Edward II granted a charter to hold an annual fair and a weekly market, thus this agricultural centre was given the go-ahead to develop.

On the brow of the 500ft hill stands St Lawrence's church that dates from the 12th century. Originally it was never intended that the church should be so far away from the village. The building materials were heaped in readiness for the construction of the church near the village green but one night, so the story goes, they disappeared, reappearing on the brow of Napton hill. Thus it was decided that the church would be far better built where the materials had landed. A short distance from the church is a windmill constructed during the 1800s together with the miller's cottage. Records show that there was a mill at Napton as far back as 1543.

A footpath leads from the mill down to where the brick and tile works once stood and where many of the residents earned their living. Local clay was used for the products and after being fired, in what was claimed to be the longest kiln in Europe, the bricks and tiles were transported by narrowboats moored alongside on the Oxford Arm of the canal.

Long Itchington

A pretty pond surrounded by trees forms the centre of the village. Just off the green are a number of half-timbered houses in one of which Elizabeth I is reputed to have stayed. The tower of the church can be seen from the towpath over to the right, close to bridge No.25.

Stockton

'Stump Endosine', as it was recorded in 1272, was the name for the present-day Stockton. The development of the village during the 18th and 19th centuries was mainly due to the nearby lime and clay deposits. The Nelson Cement Works evolved during the early 19th century and some of the profits from this industry were donated to the church. This money was used to purchase a stone house that had formerly been a stable, a school teacher was employed and by 1824 33 boys and 19 girls were attending the village school.

In 1898 a pale grey stone, a mixture of shale and limestone, was excavated at the Blue Lias Pit. At about 30ft below the surface a near-perfect fossil of a brontosaurus was discovered. It measured over

'The Farm', Sawbridge

THE GRAND UNION CANAL WALK

19ft in length and it was estimated to be 20 millions years old.

Ancient Ways
Towards the end of this stage the canal is crossed by two ancient routes. The first is at bridge No.30 where the old drovers' road, used by the cattle drovers travelling from Wales to south-east England, crosses the canal. Here the canal scene is very attractive with a bridge, cottage and the aptly named Welsh Road Lock.

A little way on, the old Roman highway, the Fosse Way, is carried over the canal by the Fosse Road bridge and the lock just before bridge No.32, together with the following two, are called the Fosse Locks.

Immediately after passing under bridge No.91 turn up to the left and leave the towpath. At the road (A45T) turn right at the signpost to Wolfhampcote church, and walk along the track towards the church, crossing the cattle-grid and walking straight ahead. Go through the metal gate and follow the track round to the right. As you approach the now disused church, the old railway line, well camouflaged by the banks of trees, draws closer (left). With the farm (right) go through the gateway and walk ahead, cross the disused railway line and continue to the trees ahead. Soon a right turn will bring you across bridge No.98 over the canal.

After bridge No.91 is the Boatman Hotel (right), the restaurant of which has been likened to a riverboat. Just beyond the moorings on the left of the canal are the twin iron bridges of Braunston. At the time of writing, the towpath from here to Calcutt is in a poor state of repair and while plans are in hand to upgrade it I would not recommend its use until this has been carried out. Instead I suggest a detour is made. This increases the mileage slightly but it does provide a change of scene, and for the most part, a tarmac surface.

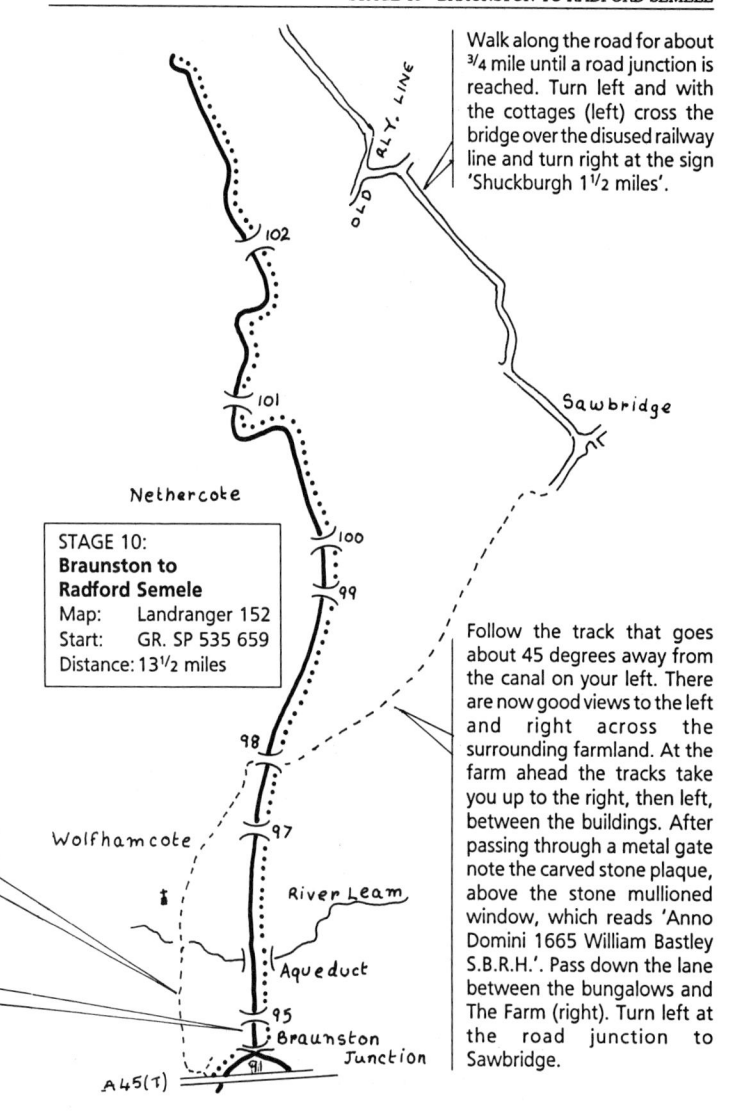

STAGE 10 - BRAUNSTON TO RADFORD SEMELE

Walk along the road for about ¾ mile until a road junction is reached. Turn left and with the cottages (left) cross the bridge over the disused railway line and turn right at the sign 'Shuckburgh 1½ miles'.

STAGE 10:
Braunston to Radford Semele
Map: Landranger 152
Start: GR. SP 535 659
Distance: 13½ miles

Follow the track that goes about 45 degrees away from the canal on your left. There are now good views to the left and right across the surrounding farmland. At the farm ahead the tracks take you up to the right, then left, between the buildings. After passing through a metal gate note the carved stone plaque, above the stone mullioned window, which reads 'Anno Domini 1665 William Bastley S.B.R.H.'. Pass down the lane between the bungalows and The Farm (right). Turn left at the road junction to Sawbridge.

THE GRAND UNION CANAL WALK

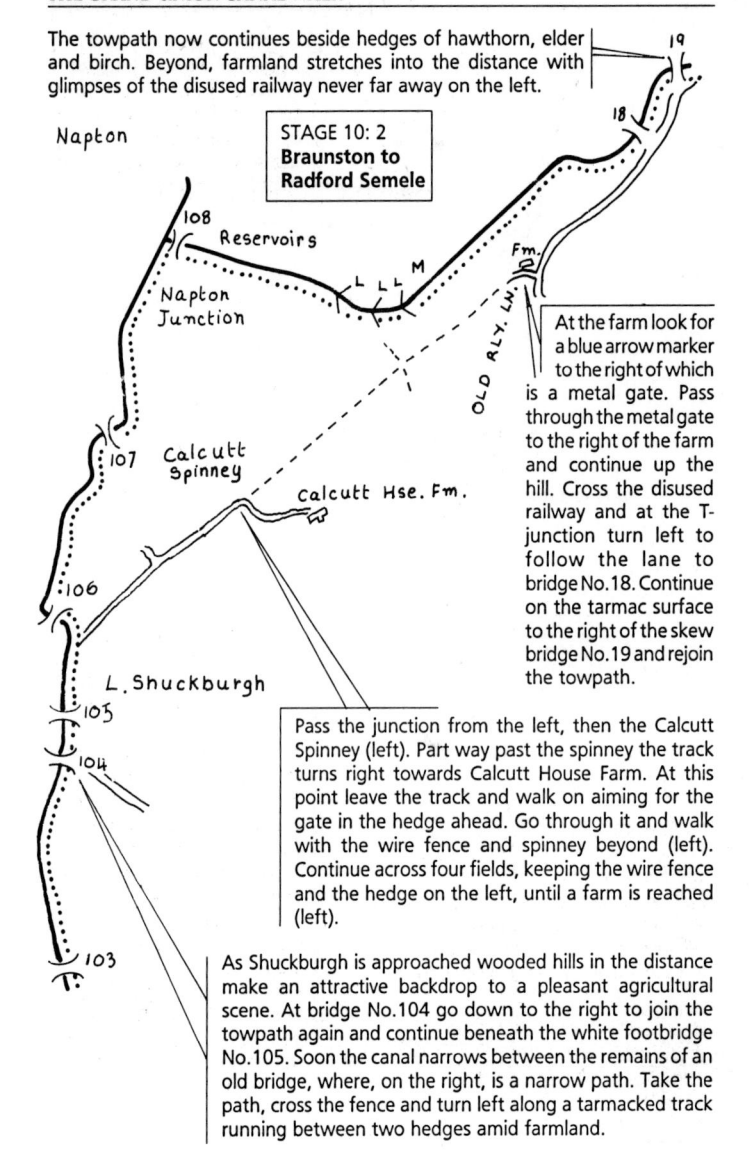

The towpath now continues beside hedges of hawthorn, elder and birch. Beyond, farmland stretches into the distance with glimpses of the disused railway never far away on the left.

**STAGE 10: 2
Braunston to
Radford Semele**

At the farm look for a blue arrow marker to the right of which is a metal gate. Pass through the metal gate to the right of the farm and continue up the hill. Cross the disused railway and at the T-junction turn left to follow the lane to bridge No.18. Continue on the tarmac surface to the right of the skew bridge No.19 and rejoin the towpath.

Pass the junction from the left, then the Calcutt Spinney (left). Part way past the spinney the track turns right towards Calcutt House Farm. At this point leave the track and walk on aiming for the gate in the hedge ahead. Go through it and walk with the wire fence and spinney beyond (left). Continue across four fields, keeping the wire fence and the hedge on the left, until a farm is reached (left).

As Shuckburgh is approached wooded hills in the distance make an attractive backdrop to a pleasant agricultural scene. At bridge No.104 go down to the right to join the towpath again and continue beneath the white footbridge No.105. Soon the canal narrows between the remains of an old bridge, where, on the right, is a narrow path. Take the path, cross the fence and turn left along a tarmacked track running between two hedges amid farmland.

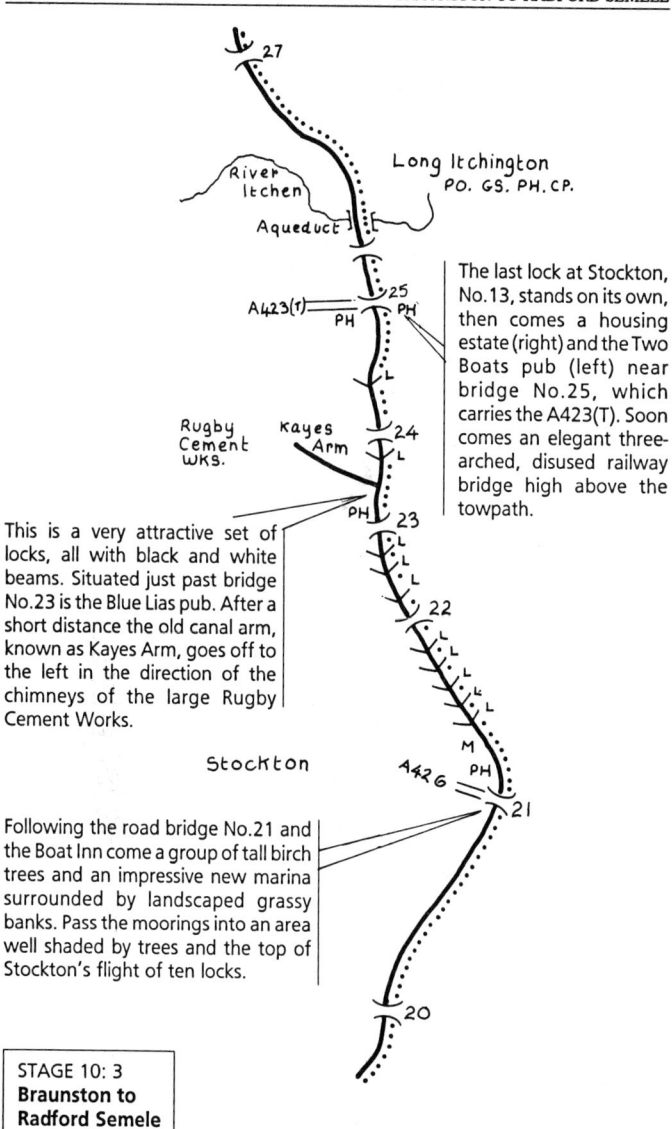

STAGE 10 - BRAUNSTON TO RADFORD SEMELE

Long Itchington
PO. GS. PH. CP.

River Itchen

Aqueduct

A423(T)

Rugby Cement Wks.

Kayes Arm

The last lock at Stockton, No.13, stands on its own, then comes a housing estate (right) and the Two Boats pub (left) near bridge No.25, which carries the A423(T). Soon comes an elegant three-arched, disused railway bridge high above the towpath.

This is a very attractive set of locks, all with black and white beams. Situated just past bridge No.23 is the Blue Lias pub. After a short distance the old canal arm, known as Kayes Arm, goes off to the left in the direction of the chimneys of the large Rugby Cement Works.

Stockton

A426

Following the road bridge No.21 and the Boat Inn come a group of tall birch trees and an impressive new marina surrounded by landscaped grassy banks. Pass the moorings into an area well shaded by trees and the top of Stockton's flight of ten locks.

STAGE 10: 3
Braunston to Radford Semele

THE GRAND UNION CANAL WALK

The canal now passes through the remainder of the Fosse Locks but before reaching the bottom lock at Radford it passes beneath the graceful brick arches of a disused viaduct. This viaduct once carried the L.N.W.R. from Rugby to Leamington. Ahead the road passes over bridge No.34 and alongside the opposite bank is a floating restaurant, The Prince Regent the Second.

Beyond bridge No.31 the canal bends left then right and from the towpath there are pleasant views across farmland (right). Trees dip into the water on the opposite bank and underfoot is a broad well-clipped towpath - easy on the feet. After Fosse Top Lock the towpath has high hedges (right) and both sides of this straight section of the canal are well wooded.

The attractive modern bridge No.27 follows traditional lines. Continue to the four Bascote Locks, as attractive in black and white as those at Stockton. After bridge No.29 the canal is lined with clumps of reed and bulrushes. Just before bridge No.30 is the Welsh Road Lock with a fairly new lock keeper's cottage across the canal.

**STAGE 10: 4
Braunston to
Radford Semele**

STAGE 11:
Radford Semele to Shrewley

PLACES AND POINTS OF INTEREST ALONG THE WAY

Radford Semele

An explanation for this unusually named Warwickshire village is that it came from a description of a 'Reeded Ford' where the River Leam could be crossed; further, Henry de Simely was the Norman landowner during the time of Henry I and by combining 'Reeded Ford' and 'Simely' we have Radford Semele. As recently as 1968 flints and axes dating from 30,000 years ago were discovered locally together with Roman coins, thereby giving evidence of settlements in the locality dating back to well before the founding of today's pleasant village.

The village church is one of the oldest buildings in the village having probably been rebuilt during the 1100s. The original church existed before the Norman Conquest but today's church, which is well away from the village, is much as the Victorians left it.

A group of travelling Huguenots are said to have completed the fine wood carvings at Radford Hall during 1622. The hall was rebuilt during Victorian times and has recently been separated into several dwellings. Radford Hall was at one time a thriving brewery, its ale becoming something of a local speciality. It survived from 1900 until it was taken over and closed down in 1969. The canal was opened, as part of the Warwick and Napton Canal, a hundred years before the founding of the local brewery.

Hampton

To the west of Warwick on 18th August 1642, just before the start of the Civil War, an 'encounter' took place at Grove Park, the home of the Catholic Royalist Robert Dormer, 1st Earl of Caernarfon. Little else of any significance seems to have happened here.

The Royal Warwickshire Regiment has strong connections with the nearby church of St Michael's at Budbrooke. This was their garrison church and the regimental colour (an antelope on a blue background) hangs close to the memorial tablet on the north wall.

THE GRAND UNION CANAL WALK

Boaters and backpackers near the top of the famous "Hatton Flight"

STAGE 11 - RADFORD SEMELE TO SHREWLEY

STAGE 11:
Radford Semele to Shrewley
Map: Landranger 151
Start: GR. SP 352 649
Distance: 10 miles

A modern Kwik Save shopping centre is on the right near bridge No.41. The canal then bends left and the surroundings become a little more pleasant, but the noise of the traffic still intrudes. The towpath now has a gravel surface as we draw level with the Leamington Plant of Ford Motor Works (right).

British Telecom is on the right before bridge No.40 and across the canal is The Bridge and row upon row of terraced houses. Then comes the Grand Union Hotel and the Canal House dated 1820 (left), which still retains some of its wrought iron balconies.

At bridge No.37, with The Fusilier and shops (left) there is a notice 'Leamington Spa ½ mile'.

The canal widens as it passes through an industrial area with rows of terraced houses and a Victorian school building. St Mary's Landing is on the left near bridge No.38 closely followed by a railway bridge. Here the air is filled with the noise of industry.

Woodland surrounds the canal and towpath and the River Leam runs alongside (right). In places the bare faces of rock can be seen where the canal has been hewn out of the hillside. After a bend in the canal, pine trees and rhododendron bushes take their place amid the surrounding woodland. The scene then changes, we enter suburbia and on the right is scrubby wasteland. In the distance can be seen the high rise buildings of Leamington Spa (right) and the Radford Semele church tower (left).

The old Thornley Brewery is on the left at Bridge No.35 and after crossing a small aqueduct there are houses on both sides of the canal. The newer houses (left) have grassy banks and canalside walkways while the gardens of the older ones reach down to the hedge at the side of the towpath.

101

THE GRAND UNION CANAL WALK

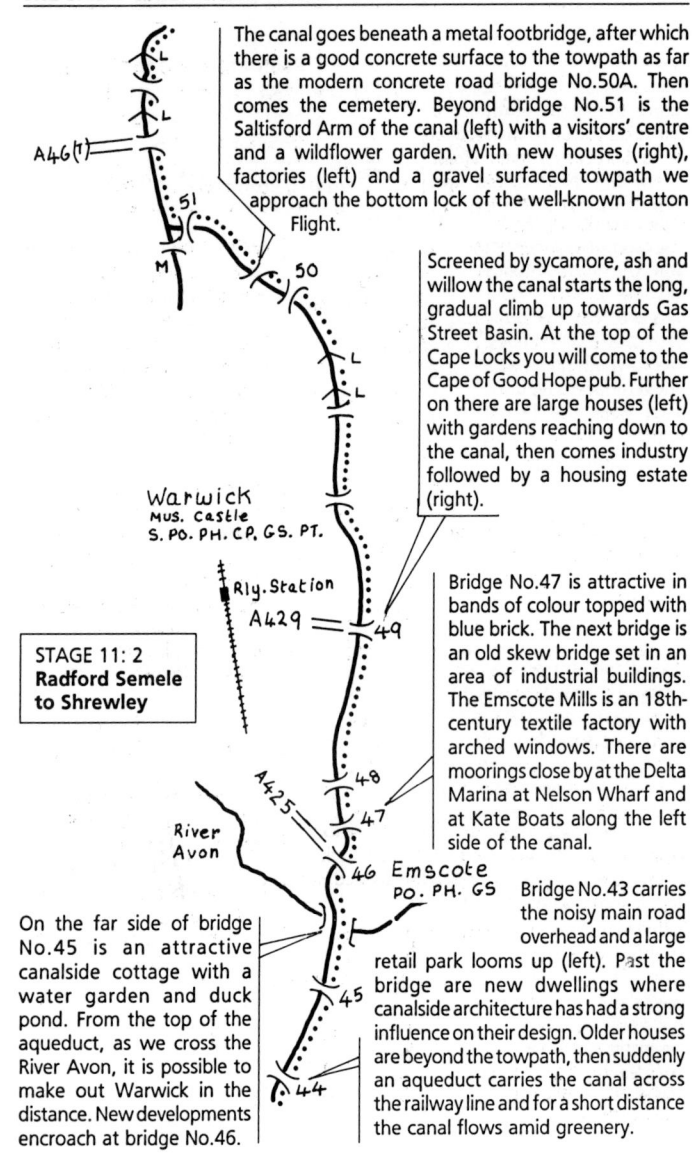

The canal goes beneath a metal footbridge, after which there is a good concrete surface to the towpath as far as the modern concrete road bridge No.50A. Then comes the cemetery. Beyond bridge No.51 is the Saltisford Arm of the canal (left) with a visitors' centre and a wildflower garden. With new houses (right), factories (left) and a gravel surfaced towpath we approach the bottom lock of the well-known Hatton Flight.

Screened by sycamore, ash and willow the canal starts the long, gradual climb up towards Gas Street Basin. At the top of the Cape Locks you will come to the Cape of Good Hope pub. Further on there are large houses (left) with gardens reaching down to the canal, then comes industry followed by a housing estate (right).

STAGE 11: 2
Radford Semele to Shrewley

Bridge No.47 is attractive in bands of colour topped with blue brick. The next bridge is an old skew bridge set in an area of industrial buildings. The Emscote Mills is an 18th-century textile factory with arched windows. There are moorings close by at the Delta Marina at Nelson Wharf and at Kate Boats along the left side of the canal.

On the far side of bridge No.45 is an attractive canalside cottage with a water garden and duck pond. From the top of the aqueduct, as we cross the River Avon, it is possible to make out Warwick in the distance. New developments encroach at bridge No.46.

Bridge No.43 carries the noisy main road overhead and a large retail park looms up (left). Past the bridge are new dwellings where canalside architecture has had a strong influence on their design. Older houses are beyond the towpath, then suddenly an aqueduct carries the canal across the railway line and for a short distance the canal flows amid greenery.

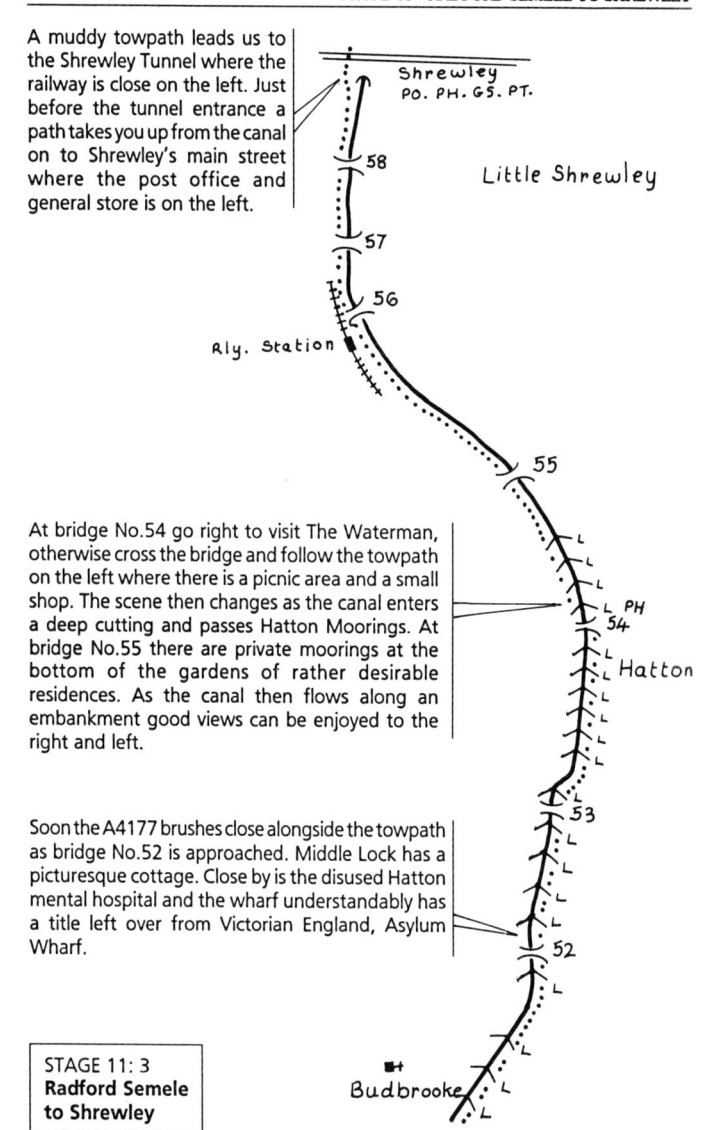

STAGE 11 - RADFORD SEMELE TO SHREWLEY

A muddy towpath leads us to the Shrewley Tunnel where the railway is close on the left. Just before the tunnel entrance a path takes you up from the canal on to Shrewley's main street where the post office and general store is on the left.

Shrewley PO. PH. GS. PT.

Little Shrewley

Rly. Station

At bridge No.54 go right to visit The Waterman, otherwise cross the bridge and follow the towpath on the left where there is a picnic area and a small shop. The scene then changes as the canal enters a deep cutting and passes Hatton Moorings. At bridge No.55 there are private moorings at the bottom of the gardens of rather desirable residences. As the canal then flows along an embankment good views can be enjoyed to the right and left.

Hatton

Soon the A4177 brushes close alongside the towpath as bridge No.52 is approached. Middle Lock has a picturesque cottage. Close by is the disused Hatton mental hospital and the wharf understandably has a title left over from Victorian England, Asylum Wharf.

STAGE 11: 3
Radford Semele to Shrewley

Budbrooke

103

STAGE 12:
Shrewley to Catherine de Barnes

PLACES AND POINTS OF INTEREST ALONG THE WAY

Shrewley
This part of Warwickshire sits on the very fringes of Shakespeare country and is often referred to as the 'Heart of England', being about as far away from the sea as any other place in the country. At the village of Shrewley the canal runs directly beneath the main street by way of the 433 yard long tunnel.

Hatton
Hatton is better known than Shrewley purely because of its flight of 21 locks close to the top of which stands the Waterman Inn.

Haseley
To the north at Haseley the lovely old church with its Norman knave, 13th-century chancel and tower dating from the 15th century seem to live in a far different world to that of the canalside villages.

Rowington
In the past the Forest of Arden covered much of this area and the original village was formed as a result of the gathering together of several scattered hamlets. 'Hrocingatun' was the Saxon name for the local settlement and later, during the Domesday survey, it was named 'Rochintone'. Several timber-framed houses remain as a reminder of the past, together with the forest and Shakespeare Hall. The hall, claimed to be the home of a branch of the bard's family, is perhaps the most significant piece of local architecture.

Royal Leamington Spa
When it was opened in 1819 the Regent Hotel was the largest in England. It was designed to cope with the ever increasing numbers of those who flocked to Leamington to take the 'waters'. So fashionable had the habit become, following the visit of Queen Victoria, that the word 'Royal' was added to the town's name in

STAGE 12 - SHREWLEY TO CATHERINE DE BARNES

The bottom lock at Knowle

1838.

The springs had been discovered late in the 16th century and a local doctor by the name of Jephson did more than most to give credibility to the apparent benefits of drinking from these saline springs. There were originally seven such spring and in 1814 a pump room was built over one of these water sources.

John Nash had much to do with the building of Leamington. The town has fine examples of terraces constructed during some of the most elegant periods of England's architectural development.

Warwick

For me, Warwick is one of the most inviting places along this route. It is a blend of the grand magnificence of Medieval and Georgian architecture. However, the canal and towpath to which the walker is committed slices through a lesser known part of the town.

Warwick Castle was rebuilt in the 14th century on an old site that Henry de Newburgh had acquired from William the Conqueror. For almost 600 years this was the seat of the Earls of Warwick. It has a history closely associated with the development of this country: from grim faced, forbidding, deep, grisly dungeons to grand state apartments reflecting the grandeur of England.

Beyond the castle walls the beautiful old Lord Leycester Hospital dates from the 12th and 16th centuries. It has in its time been used as a guildhall, council chamber and a grammar school.

The church of St Mary's has Norman connections and was given collegiate status by Roger, Earl of Warwick, in 1123. This meant that it was to be regarded as a cathedral. Unfortunately during the late 17th century a fire destroyed much of the old building.

Fine examples of Warwick's later development are to be seen in Northgate Street. Here are buildings in the Classic style, perhaps the finest being the Shire Hall with its two octagonal courtrooms.

The most attractive viewpoint of Warwick is from the 18th-century Castle Bridge that spans the River Arden on the south side of the town.

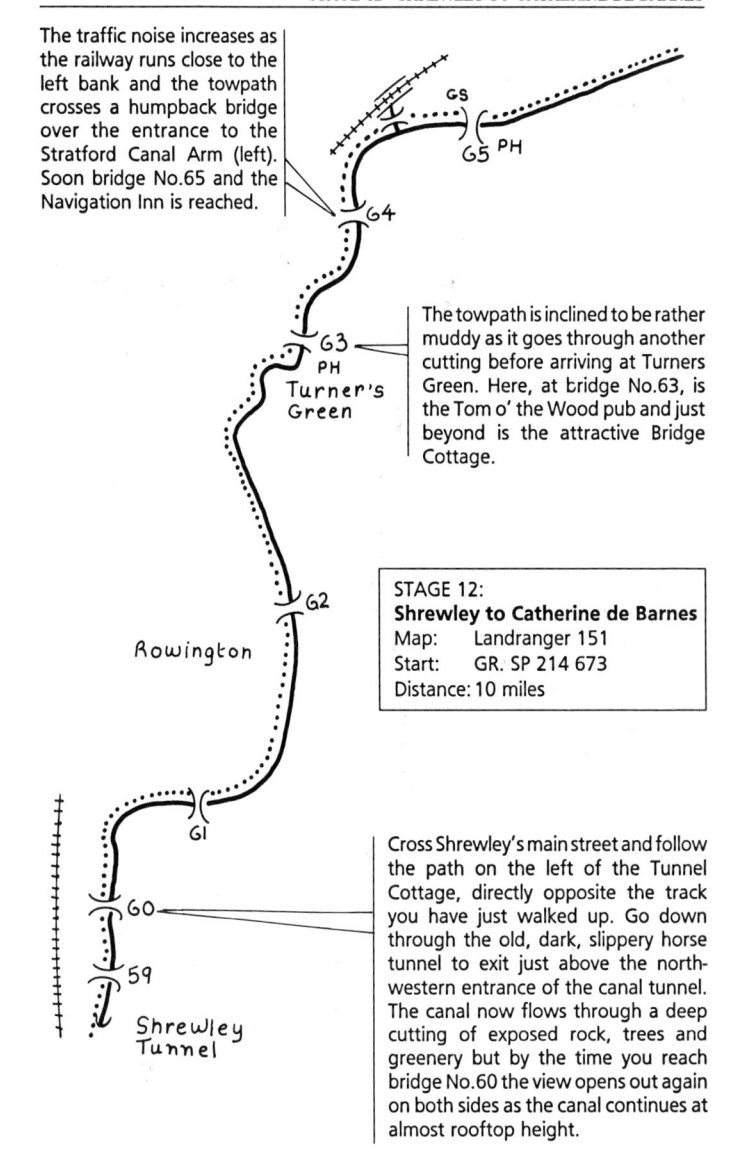

STAGE 12 - SHREWLEY TO CATHERINE DE BARNES

The traffic noise increases as the railway runs close to the left bank and the towpath crosses a humpback bridge over the entrance to the Stratford Canal Arm (left). Soon bridge No.65 and the Navigation Inn is reached.

The towpath is inclined to be rather muddy as it goes through another cutting before arriving at Turners Green. Here, at bridge No.63, is the Tom o' the Wood pub and just beyond is the attractive Bridge Cottage.

STAGE 12:
Shrewley to Catherine de Barnes
Map: Landranger 151
Start: GR. SP 214 673
Distance: 10 miles

Cross Shrewley's main street and follow the path on the left of the Tunnel Cottage, directly opposite the track you have just walked up. Go down through the old, dark, slippery horse tunnel to exit just above the north-western entrance of the canal tunnel. The canal now flows through a deep cutting of exposed rock, trees and greenery but by the time you reach bridge No.60 the view opens out again on both sides as the canal continues at almost rooftop height.

107

THE GRAND UNION CANAL WALK

STAGE 12: 2
**Shrewley to
Catherine de Barnes**

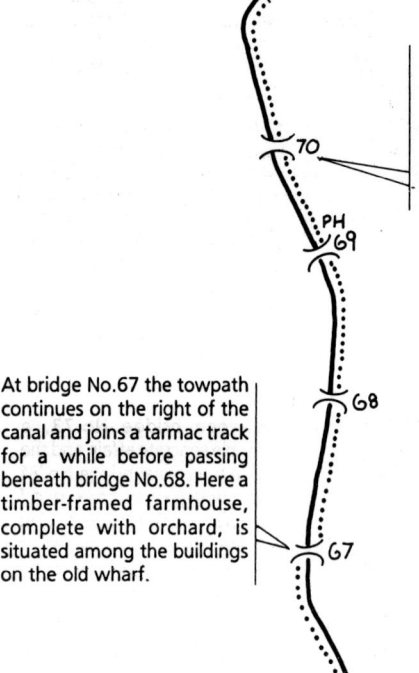

The renovated Black Boy pub is adjacent to bridge No.69. After bridge No.70 Knowle Hill, dotted with trees, comes into view and as you proceed the Knowle Locks can be seen ascending in the distance.

At bridge No.67 the towpath continues on the right of the canal and joins a tarmac track for a while before passing beneath bridge No.68. Here a timber-framed farmhouse, complete with orchard, is situated among the buildings on the old wharf.

The division marker between the Severn and Trent River Authorities is on the wall of bridge No.66.

66 PH. PO. PT.
Baddesley
Clinton 3/4 m ▶

108

STAGE 12 - SHREWLEY TO CATHERINE DE BARNES

STAGE 12: 3
Shrewley to Catherine de Barnes

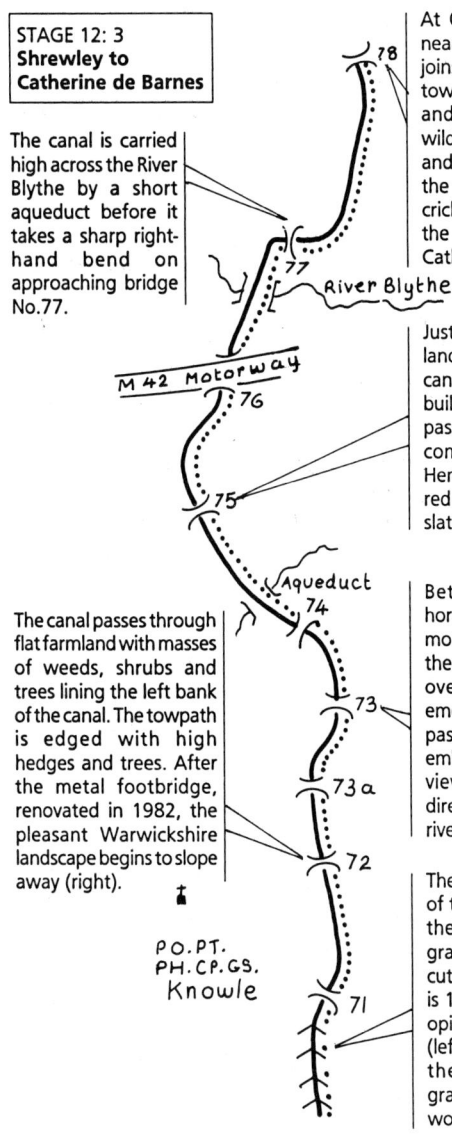

The canal is carried high across the River Blythe by a short aqueduct before it takes a sharp right-hand bend on approaching bridge No.77.

At Oak Farm, a poultry farm near bridge No.78, the towpath joins a tarmac driveway. The towpath is clothed with ferns and on the opposite bank wildflowers, ferns, oak, willow and hawthorn reach down to the water's edge. Further on a cricket ground is on the left of the canal. We have arrived at Catherine de Barnes.

Just beyond bridge No.75 the landscape on both sides of the canal is pleasant with farm buildings up to the left. After passing beneath the M42 you come to the moorings of Henwood Wharf where the red brick canal cottage has a slate roof.

The canal passes through flat farmland with masses of weeds, shrubs and trees lining the left bank of the canal. The towpath is edged with high hedges and trees. After the metal footbridge, renovated in 1982, the pleasant Warwickshire landscape begins to slope away (right).

PO.PT.
PH.CP.GS.
Knowle

Between bridge No.73, a horrible concrete affair, and the more traditional bridge No.74 the towpath is very narrow and overhung with nettles. On emerging from the cutting it passes along the top of an embankment from where good views can be had in both directions as it passes over a river.

The towpath passes to the right of these colourful locks where there are flower beds and grassed areas as the top of the cutting is reached. From here it is 13 miles to Gas Street. Canopied buildings line the wharf (left). Beyond the road bridge the walls of the cutting gradually disappear to reveal woodland again.

109

STAGE 13:
Catherine de Barnes to Gas Street Basin

PLACES AND POINTS OF INTEREST ALONG THE WAY

Solihull

It is difficult to believe now, but at the time of the Domesday survey the area known today as Solihull was one of the most sparsely populated areas in England. By 1220 the church of St Alphege was founded and 22 years later the village of Solihull was granted a charter to hold a local market once a week.

Today the centre of Solihull still has a few timber-framed buildings left from Tudor England and what there are have become part of a conglomeration of buildings from different periods and reflecting different styles of architecture.

The Old Berry Hall dates from the 15th century and the George Inn is still attractive. Otherwise the sprawl of Birmingham has reached its edges but has, as yet, not completely encompassed Solihull.

Birmingham

While Birmingham is not as world renowned for its canals as is Venice, it does have more miles of waterway. Mainly constructed during the 18th and 19th centuries they provide a magnificent system of transportation right into the heart of one of the world's most important engineering centres.

During the Industrial Revolution the city's development was second to none and so it has remained for many generations, being noted especially for mechanical engineering and metal work. Going back even earlier, to the English Civil War, the town was said to have equipped the Parliamentarians with 15,000 swords, a very hefty order in those days.

The Birmingham Canal was built by James Brindley in 1769 with the prime task of transporting coal from Wednesbury. This canal met up with the Worcester Canal and the Fazely Canal and later the Grand Union connected with the Fazely at Gravely Hill.

Many of the old canals are still preserved and this will become

Through dark, damp tunnels and over well worn cobbles the towpath climbs up toward Gas Street Basin

apparent as you get closer to the city centre. At Gas Street Basin there are numerous mooring facilities for cabin cruisers and traditional narrowboats. Trips along the canal run all year round from Kingston Row and Gas Street and there are canalside walks, if you haven't already had enough of walking by the time you arrive here.

Birmingham has a good variety of museums and galleries and some fine architecture although it is quite spread out. The Bull Ring is the traditional centre where markets have been held since the 12th century. At the time of writing a great deal of construction work is going on in this vicinity. Hopefully the new developments will be a great improvement.

St Philip's is the city's Anglican cathedral, only gaining cathedral status in 1905 although it was consecrated in 1715. Thomas Archer, the architect, was influenced by the Baroque style and this is reflected in the building. St Chad's, completed in 1841, was the first Roman Catholic cathedral to be built in England since the Reformation. It was designed by Augustus Pugin (one of the architects of the Houses of Parliament) but the best known of the city's churches is the 13th-century St Martin's, situated at the Bull Ring.

THE GRAND UNION CANAL WALK

Gas Street Basin, Birmingham

STAGE 13 - CATHERINE DE BARNES TO GAS STREET BASIN

THE GRAND UNION CANAL WALK

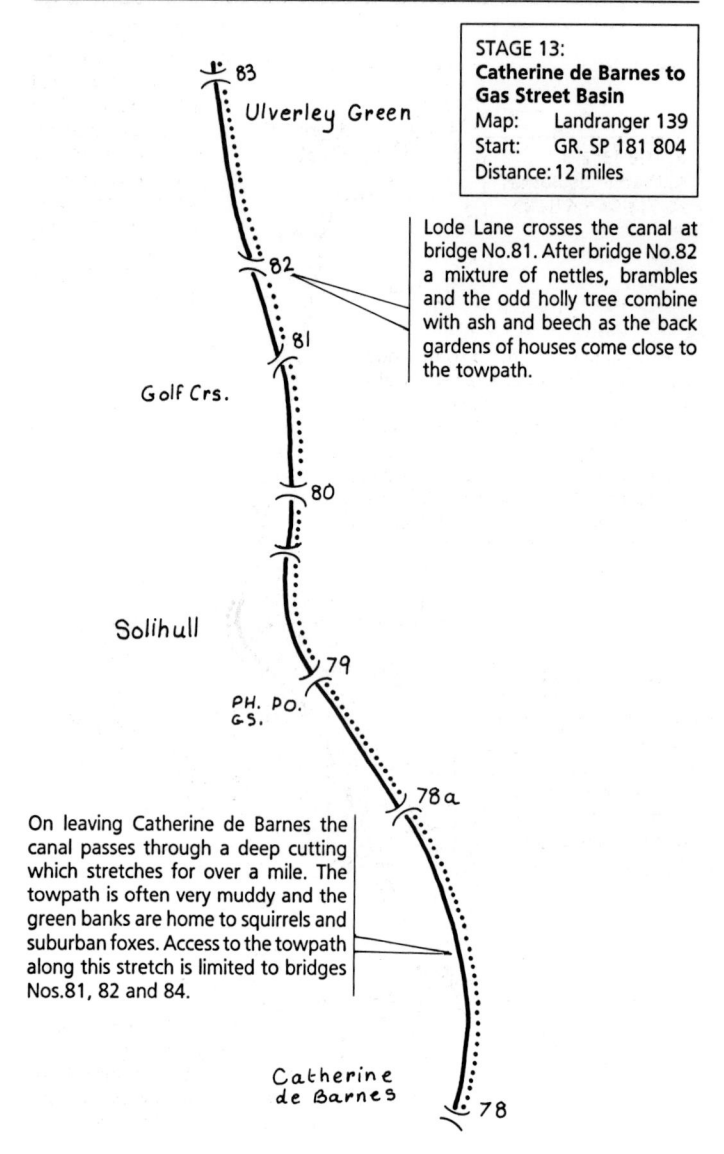

> STAGE 13:
> **Catherine de Barnes to Gas Street Basin**
> Map: Landranger 139
> Start: GR. SP 181 804
> Distance: 12 miles

Lode Lane crosses the canal at bridge No.81. After bridge No.82 a mixture of nettles, brambles and the odd holly tree combine with ash and beech as the back gardens of houses come close to the towpath.

Ulverley Green

Golf Crs.

Solihull

PH. PO. GS.

On leaving Catherine de Barnes the canal passes through a deep cutting which stretches for over a mile. The towpath is often very muddy and the green banks are home to squirrels and suburban foxes. Access to the towpath along this stretch is limited to bridges Nos.81, 82 and 84.

Catherine de Barnes

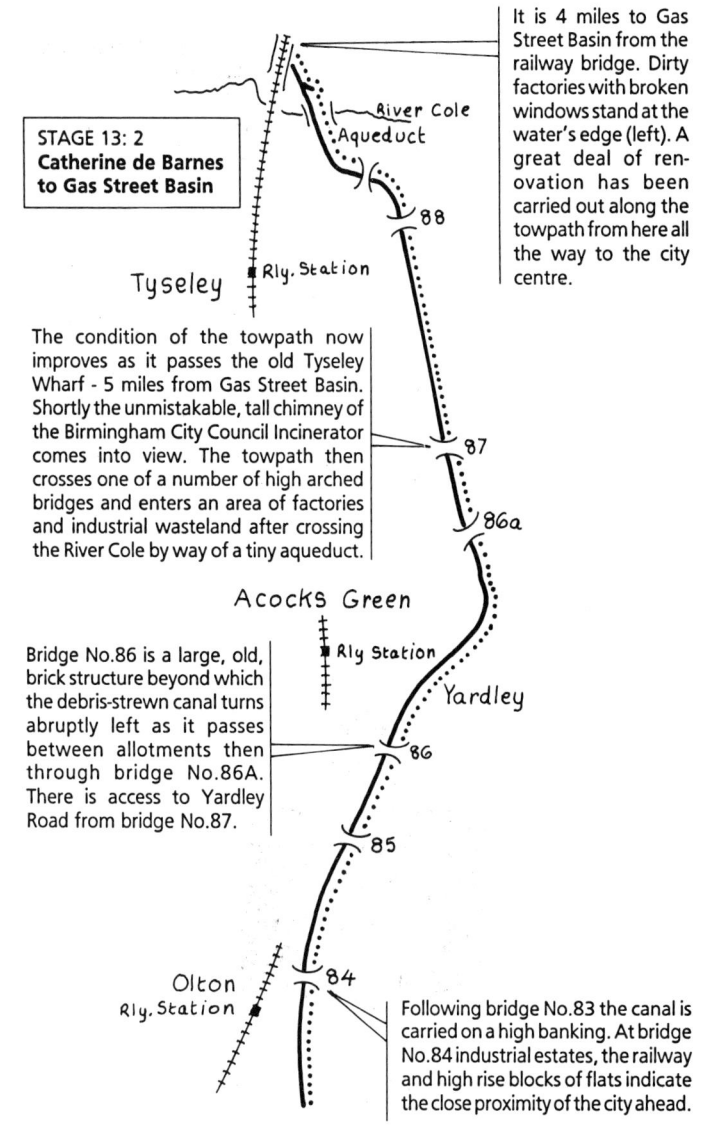

STAGE 13 - CATHERINE DE BARNES TO GAS STREET BASIN

It is 4 miles to Gas Street Basin from the railway bridge. Dirty factories with broken windows stand at the water's edge (left). A great deal of renovation has been carried out along the towpath from here all the way to the city centre.

STAGE 13: 2 Catherine de Barnes to Gas Street Basin

River Cole Aqueduct

Tyseley — Rly. Station

The condition of the towpath now improves as it passes the old Tyseley Wharf - 5 miles from Gas Street Basin. Shortly the unmistakable, tall chimney of the Birmingham City Council Incinerator comes into view. The towpath then crosses one of a number of high arched bridges and enters an area of factories and industrial wasteland after crossing the River Cole by way of a tiny aqueduct.

Acocks Green
Rly Station

Yardley

Bridge No.86 is a large, old, brick structure beyond which the debris-strewn canal turns abruptly left as it passes between allotments then through bridge No.86A. There is access to Yardley Road from bridge No.87.

Olton Rly. Station

Following bridge No.83 the canal is carried on a high banking. At bridge No.84 industrial estates, the railway and high rise blocks of flats indicate the close proximity of the city ahead.

115

THE GRAND UNION CANAL WALK

STAGE 13: 3
Catherine de Barnes to Gas Street Basin

Keeping to the left, the Hyatt Hotel, followed by the ultra modern, aptly named James Brindley pub, soon appears amid the old, converted canalside warehouses.

Bearing left continue to the iron and brick Barker Bridge, dated 1842. Here it is 1¼ miles to Gas Street Basin. The Salvation Army Centre is next (left) then Snow Hill and the first of the thirteen locks of the Farmer's Flight. Pass beneath the massive brick arch of the old railway bridge where the towpath continues uphill, past the base of the British Telecom Tower (left) then under bridges and beside the locks until the Cambrian Wharf, at the top of the locks, is reached.

This is journey's end at Gas Street Basin.
Congratulations!

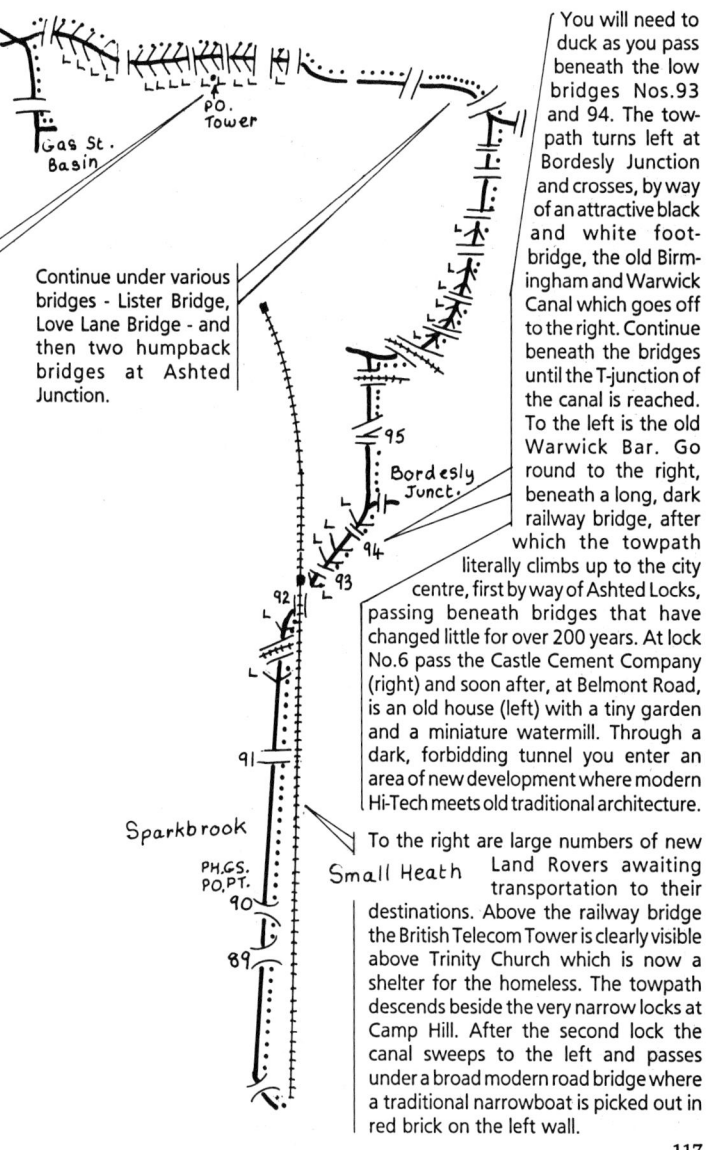

STAGE 13 - CATHERINE DE BARNES TO GAS STREET BASIN

You will need to duck as you pass beneath the low bridges Nos.93 and 94. The towpath turns left at Bordesly Junction and crosses, by way of an attractive black and white footbridge, the old Birmingham and Warwick Canal which goes off to the right. Continue beneath the bridges until the T-junction of the canal is reached. To the left is the old Warwick Bar. Go round to the right, beneath a long, dark railway bridge, after which the towpath literally climbs up to the city centre, first by way of Ashted Locks, passing beneath bridges that have changed little for over 200 years. At lock No.6 pass the Castle Cement Company (right) and soon after, at Belmont Road, is an old house (left) with a tiny garden and a miniature watermill. Through a dark, forbidding tunnel you enter an area of new development where modern Hi-Tech meets old traditional architecture.

To the right are large numbers of new Land Rovers awaiting transportation to their destinations. Above the railway bridge the British Telecom Tower is clearly visible above Trinity Church which is now a shelter for the homeless. The towpath descends beside the very narrow locks at Camp Hill. After the second lock the canal sweeps to the left and passes under a broad modern road bridge where a traditional narrowboat is picked out in red brick on the left wall.

Continue under various bridges - Lister Bridge, Love Lane Bridge - and then two humpback bridges at Ashted Junction.

USEFUL ADDRESSES

TOURIST INFORMATION CENTRES

London Tourist Board: 26 Grosvenor Gardens, London SW1 0DU. Tel: 0171 730 3488.

Rickmansworth: Three Rivers House, Northway, Rickmansworth, Herts WD3 1RL. Tel: 01923 776611 ext 1381.

Hemel Hempstead: Pavilion Box Office, Marlowes, Hemel Hempstead, Herts HP1 1HA. Tel: 01442 64451.

Berkhamsted: The Library, 26 Kings Road, Berkhamsted, Herts HP4 3BD. Tel: 01442 877638.

Milton Keynes: 536 Silbury Boulevard, Milton Keynes, Bucks MK9 3AF. Tel: 01908 232525.

Daventry: Moot Hall, Market Square, Daventry, Northants NN11 4BH. Tel: 01327 300277.

Leamington Spa: Jephson Lodge, Jephson Gardens, The Parade, Leamington Spa, Warwickshire CV32 4AB. Tel: 01926 311470.

Warwick: The Court House, Jury Street, Warwick, Warwickshire CV34 4EW. Tel: 01926 492212.

Birmingham: Convention and Visitor Bureau, 2 City Arcade, Birmingham, West Midlands B2 4TX. Tel: 0121 643 2514.

Solihull: Central Library, Homer Road, West Midlands B91 3RG. Tel: 0121 704 6130/6134.

Youth Hostel Association: England and Wales, Trevelyan House, 8 St Stephen's Hill, St Albans, Herts AL1 2DT.

RAIL ENQUIRIES

Bletchley (also for MK, L/Buzzard and Wolverton)
01908 370883
High Wycombe (Marylebone Line)
01494 441561
Watford Junction
01923 245001
London (Euston/Marylebone)
0171 387 7070
London (Paddington)
0171 262 6767
London (Kings X/St Pancras)
0171 278 2477
L/Buzzard
01908 644916
Milton Keynes
01908 648624
Bletchley
01908 648596

BUS SERVICES

National Express, London
0171 730 0202
London, Victoria Coach Station
0171 730 3466
Milton Keynes
01908 692416
Northampton
01604 24544
Birmingham
0121 622 4372

TRAVEL SERVICES

London Transport
0171 222 1234
Green Line/London Country
01923 673121

Milton Keynes Citibus
01908 668366
Alder Valley: High Wycombe
01494 20941
Buffalo Travel: Leighton Buzzard
01525 712132